KEEPING THE DRE.

KEEPING THE DREAM ALIVE

A sequel to 'LILAC AND ROSES' by Peggy Anderson

JAN BEVAN

ISBN
1 901253 48 1
First published March 2005

Published by:
Léonie Press
an imprint of
Anne Loader Publications
13 Vale Road, Hartford,
Northwich, Cheshire CW8 1PL Gt Britain
Tel: 01606 75660   Fax: 01606 77609
e-mail: anne@leoniepress.com
Website: www.anneloaderpublications.co.uk
www.leoniepress.com

Design and layout by: Anne Loader Publications
Covers laminated by: The Finishing Touch, St Helens
Printed by: MRT @3D www.mrtresponse.com

Cover photographs of Peggy and Alan (1976), Jan and Mike (2004)
on the steps of La Clède by Christina Anderson

Dedicated to Mike Kay,
"mon homme exceptionnel",
who helped me to fulfil so many
of Peg's dreams and my own.

CONTENTS

ILLUSTRATIONS

PREFACE

THE DREAM of the title is my mum's – simply to have a home in a beautiful part of France and the pleasure of living in it – and with the French – for a large part of the year. Mike and I are certainly keeping this alive! The book was written in celebration of the Anderson family's forty years in the Ardèche, and of La Clède's ten years as a *gîte*, as well as being a record of the work done to the house, firstly with my parents, Peggy and Alan, and then with Mike. (Just skip the descriptions of the DIY if it's not your thing!) I certainly couldn't have done it all without them, especially Mike.

As a Baby Boomer, I grew up with some of the best popular and alternative music ever. I'm a huge fan of so many British and American rock musicians, especially guitarists, but my two biggest heroes happen to be North American – Bob Dylan and Joni Mitchell (Canadian, to be specific), because they both "love words". In fact, I wanted to quote a number of Joni Mitchell lyrics throughout the book – they seemed so fitting as I was writing this in 2003 – but her music publishers finally refused authorisation at the beginning of October 2004 with no explanation given. She was yet another reason to celebrate as she was sixty last year on 7 November. I just love coincidences, and find it extremely bizarre, for instance, that our maiden names are so similar – she was born Roberta Joan Anderson and her close friends call her Joan – and that our fathers both played trumpet. (I could go on but won't!) Other JM fanatics may recognise a few references, and I list her twenty-three albums at the end for anyone who may like to discover more of her music. To me, as for so many of her fans, she's always seemed to be an absent friend and kindred spirit.

One of Mike's and my favourite ongoing games is Song Titles, naming the performers, and, even more difficult, the year! There are song titles scattered throughout the book. Count them if you wish, as an added distraction!

Jan Bevan
December 2004

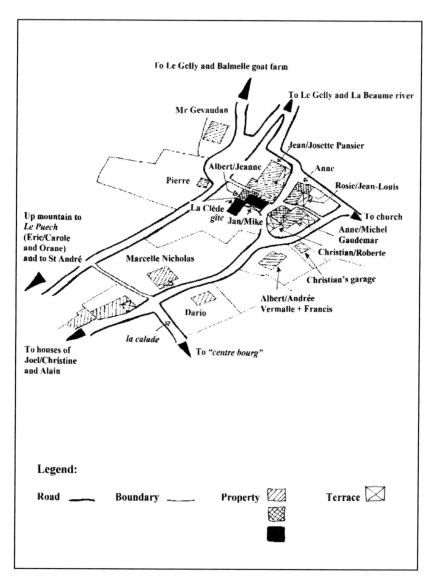

Neighbours in *Le Chauvet* hamlet

LA CLÈDE

The name of our house, *La Clède*, is the French word for the build-ing in which sweet chestnuts, once a staple part of the local diet, were preserved by drying over heat from a fire.

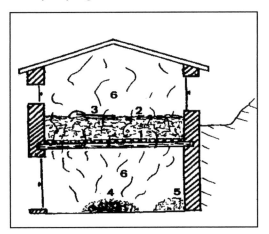

Diagram of a *clède*: 1: grille; 2: chestnuts; 3: rake; 4: fire (the nuts' husks are used as kindling and fuel; 5: ashes; 6: smoke

OUR HOME IN THE CEVENNES SUN

"SO, THE HOUSE isn't mine, then?"

My dad, Alan, looked confused, tired and grateful we'd been able to find a seat outside the crowded café. It was market day in Joyeuse and still busy, even though it was nearly midday and some of the traders had already started packing up.

"Well, it's half yours, Al. And, of course, we'll let you stay as long as you want!" I joked.

The two of us had just paid a visit to the *notaire* (solicitor) to sort out the papers on the house, which was in my late mother, Peggy's name. We were both still reeling from the concentration of listening to, and trying to comprehend, all that legal jargon in French. The waitress arrived at our table.

"I think I need a whisky," said Alan. "Are you having a *pastis*? I'll use some of your water."

"*Un scotch et un pastis, s'il vous plaît,*" I ordered.

"Things have modernised somewhat in the legal profession since 1964, haven't they?" he commented, smiling wryly.

"Yes, they've discovered filing at least!" I laughed, remembering my mother's account of her one and only visit to the *notaire*, which she had described as pure Dickensian, with mountains of dusty papers and files everywhere.

Alan and I had sat and listened to what would happen now with regard to the property, and what needed to be done next. Our *maître* had had a shock in store for Alan, as he explained the finer points of the Napoleonic laws on property inheritance. It seemed that La Clède was not to be his. He only owned a half of it, with myself and brother Ian sharing the other half, although he had the right to live there *en usufruit*, that is, until his death. He seemed rather taken aback at his newly discovered loss of sole legal control over the future of the house. More probably, though,

1

he was annoyed he'd have the chore of instructing his English lawyer to alter his will, although it was understood by us all that Ian and I would inherit 'the cottage' eventually.

We sat as if in a daze, watching the animated scene all around us. The locals had come early and left by nine or ten o'clock, to avoid the later-rising tourists still milling around on the lookout for souvenirs rather than fresh food. The Pizzas Marie van had a queue – doing well as usual. Alan seemed lost in his own thoughts. The waitress brought the drinks, and he dreamily picked up the carafe and added some water to both.

"Well, I'm blowed," he suddenly said, taking a hefty slug of his whisky. "The end of an era. Seems like it's over to you and Ian now. *Bonne* bloody *chance!*" We clinked glasses.

Alan died of a heart attack nearly two years later in April 1994.

And so it came to pass that my brother and I became *co-propriétaires* of the large, eighteenth century stone farmhouse in southern France (pictured at the beginning). Before Nippi and Nigel's story on Channel 4's *A House in the Sun* in 2002/3, most English people had never heard of the Ardèche. Forty years ago, an awful lot of French people hadn't either! My parents at that time had come to Aubenas as part of their annual French holiday and, put somewhat flippantly, they bought the house because one afternoon the Hôtel de la Pinède's tennis court was booked and they went house-hunting instead! It certainly wasn't as simple as that, as my mum, Peggy Anderson, related in *Lilac and Roses*.

It's two houses really, each roughly the same size, L-shaped, and linked by a communal door in the corner where they join each other. The property's set in about three-quarters of an acre of terraced mountain land on four levels, in a small village near Joyeuse (about 25km from Aubenas). This interesting, medieval market town is apparently named after Charlemagne's sword, Joyeuse – an odd name for a weapon, but I've certainly always been happy here! The village river is called L'Alune, (which sounds like *la lune,* meaning the moon). To a Cancerian such as I, ruled by the moon, this can seem all too fatalistic. Was it an accident or was I 'pushed' to love it so?!

The thing about La Clède is that it's never had a great deal of money poured into it – it probably shows! – just a lot of love, blood, sweat and tears! It's unbelievable to look back and see what appear to us now as the extremely low costs to my parents for the house and the work they had done. French house prices are suddenly beginning to rise fast, even in the Ardèche (once one of the lowest-cost departments along with Lozère), and you still can't get a builder's time to save your life! Northern Europeans are heading, lemming-like, towards the south and the sun, and the property market is booming.

Peggy and Alan had sold a piece of garden next to the house we all lived in, in Redhill, Surrey, for around £1,000 in 1962 and they paid 10,000F for La Clède in 1963 (when there were around 12FF or 13FF to the pound). From then on, they agreed, it was to be Peg's project. They never again had a lump sum for all the building work that was required. My mum saved like mad while she was working – sacrificing other things like a car (bussing and walking to work) and clothes which she loved. She made them instead and scoured charity shops to find bargains for herself and La Clède. And she collected books and books of Green Shield stamps!

The heavy building work in France had to be done bit by bit, according to immediate needs, rather than as a complete renovation project from scratch. It has, however, ended up being an extremely pleasant and comfortable house, and after their retirement in 1972, my parents enjoyed eighteen long summers there, usually from May to September, until 1990 when Peg was diagnosed with melanoma. Ironic a *dénouement* for such a sun-lover.

During some of those years, all three of us, Peg, Alan and I worked on the second, older half of the property – the building that actually had been used as *la clède* and which Peg had described when she first saw it in 1963 as "Cinderellaland". Much to her disappointment, the surveyor had recommended they do up the newer side and leave the side with most of the character for a future project. So, they'd literally just swept it out and used it as a general store – for wine, garden and terrace furniture and so on.

It's about the same size as the newer bit, but with only two rooms per floor instead of three. Both sides are three storeys high,

3

including cellars at lower ground level with separate entrance doors. There are external steps up to the front doors (at the accommodation ground floor level) of both houses. Like the black hole of Calcutta, the old side had once caught fire (part of the roof went up in flames), as well as having decades of smoke on the stone walls from chestnut-drying. The first jobs Peg had grudgingly had to pay for were a new roof on the part of the property they weren't even going to live in (to stop it falling down), and replacing a dangerous, rotten wooden floor in the far ground floor room with a cheap concrete one.

In spring 1977, on an impulse, I left my job in publicity at the Crafts Council and drove down to Ribes. I swept up the entrance ramp to greet astonished parents gardening in the courtyard – I hadn't forewarned them as I thought they'd be mad at what I'd done.

"Hi! How are you? I thought, if it's OK with you, I'd start working on the old side, tarting it up a bit."

"Well, hello, darling! How long are you planning on staying then? What about your job?" asked Peg. I recognised the shock and worry in her voice at any possible worse news to come – I hadn't been the easiest of daughters!

"Oh, I dunno. I've given up work." I hurried on to stem their reaction. "I'm sick of the rat race. You've got to work twice as hard as the blokes for less money. I thought I'd get into something physical. Hey, and guess what? I've been commissioned to write a book!* Someone at Hamiltons' kids section I met through work. I was telling her about that time I stayed on a houseboat in Amsterdam with Keith, and we found the rabbit in the canal. She suggested I write it for 4-5 year olds."

My parents' eyes widened. "Well, that's a lot of news all at once," said Peg. "Let's go and have a drink and you can fill us in some more."

---

*This must have irritated my mum. After her failure to get *Lilac and Roses* published in the mid seventies, she started writing children's stories – she'd been an infant teacher – but as yet hadn't had anything published. Needless to say, *Champion Rabbit* was never published either!

The three of us walked towards the house and up the steps to the terrace and the welcome shade of the virginia creeper. I breathed a little more easily.

"How are things here, anyway? Are you both OK and enjoying life?" I asked.

"We're fine," they both said.

"We've had some really lovely weather. It's not too hot to work in the garden." Peg continued. "We've seen some of our friends[*] – most of them haven't arrived yet, though. We keep busy, you know, with the usual things we do here."

"Well, I'm hoping to get Al using all those woodworking tools he got for a retirement present. Have you had them out of the box yet, Al?" He laughed at the mild dig. Before he could answer, Peg jumped in quickly to defend him.

"Yes, actually," she said, "he's made me some more shelves from those old floorboards we kept from next door. We've got so many books to house, I was desperate."

"Brilliant," I cried, rubbing Alan fondly on the back. "Can I commission some more?"

---

[*]These were nearly all French friends, some with *maisons secondaires* in the area. There were very few foreigners around, some Dutch and Belgians – hardly any English. Peg and Alan were the first foreigners to arrive in Ribes.

- 1 -
ABSOLUTE (DIY) BEGINNERS

LIKE the side of the property that Peg and Alan renovated, the *la clède* accommodation is also on two floors, which are linked this older side by a rickety, wooden ladder-type staircase. The access to their top floor, the *grenier* (loft), had originally only been through the rear door, one terrace level higher up, and they'd had a staircase put in. The bigger of the two rooms on the ground floor had originally been the kitchen and had probably only become the *clède* when the new house had been added on. The women would have cooked on the fire in the large chimneybreast and washed dishes in the old stone sink, built into the thick wall, its 'plug' just a hole through to the outside to let out the water.

When the change of use was required, the chimney was likely to have been reduced to rise to first floor level only to create the *clède* (see diagram at the beginning of the book). Above it they'd constructed a large grilled container supported on beams, into which the chestnuts were poured after the harvest. The fire was then lit below and the rising heat dried the nuts, the smoke also curing hams and *saucissons* in the *grenier* above. When the container and beams were destroyed in the fire, the upper floor became a mezzanine looking down on to the top of the chimney and the chimneybreast in the room below. Beyond these spaces was another room on each floor. So it wasn't a difficult job to plan the function of the rooms – the old kitchen would become the *salle de séjour* or lounge, the room beyond the kitchen/diner, the mezzanine and room above, the bedrooms and ablution areas.

That summer I made an awful lot of mess. Despite blocking the intercommunicating doorway between the two houses, my constant sanding of beams and doors, and de-plastering of walls caused continuous dust storms *chez* Peg and Alan. Peg wasn't too happy about it – or about the disruption to their peaceful retirement – but at the same time was very delighted to get something done in the part of the house she'd really fancied doing up all along. I too got covered in dirt and soot – extremely filthy in fact. I worked in a bikini and mask which when removed produced the 'porno tan' of all time! Picture it, if you will!

The solid chestnut beams and doors came beautifully back to life after sanding, treating and matt-varnishing. And the stones we discovered underneath the plaster were large and well cut. I hacked away day after day. We must have carried down well over a hundred buckets of rubble. Most of the plaster was extremely poor quality, but there were some areas in the old kitchen which I just couldn't shift. We were all real DIY amateurs, but good tryers and not averse to hard work. I used all the wrong tools – I know now about club hammers, bolsters, scrutch hammers even[*], thanks to Mike, my partner – but we were all delighted with our efforts. We'd got the ball rolling on the restoration and, by the end of the summer, we ended up with three clear rooms with walls and floors to treat – the two rooms downstairs and the smaller room above, which also had a concrete floor. Some of the floorboards upstairs in the mezzanine were in a bad way, and you had to tread very gingerly to get to the room beyond. Peg decided over her Cinzano one evening to get Dédé, the village carpenter to replace the floor in the same original style – with very wide chestnut tongue and groove planks. Then at least the whole place would be safe! And still in character.

Meanwhile, I started pointing the stones – another first for me – in the front room downstairs, which was to be the kitchen/diner. This room had another local feature – a beamed and *brique*-vaulted ceiling, which had been added along with small chimneys in two of the corners to help maintain a constantly warm temperature for silk worms. There had been a thriving silk industry in the

---

[*] Mike bought one this year – a vicious-looking, two-headed tool with thick teeth. "What's that for?" I asked. "Perfect for taking plaster off walls." "Twenty-five years too late, dear!"

region until the early nineteenth century, and many houses had had their own *magnagnerie* (silk house).

The property's original silk house had stood in what is now the courtyard. It was a complete ruin when my parents bought the place, and they'd had it demolished to give themselves a view and a drive-in parking area.

This older part of the property was well built originally, which is quite obvious when you see the beautifully dressed stones of the wall at the foot of the entrance ramp. We were told by neighbours that some of the door and window stones were likely taken from a local *château* or church soon after the Revolution, which dates its construction to late eighteenth century. Our immediate predecessors had obviously fallen on hard times, hadn't been able to afford to repair their buildings and had used what was available and still intact for their needs. Indeed, some original stone mullions from the windows on this façade had been removed to sell, which only confirms how desperately in need of money they were. In *Lilac and Roses*, Peg describes the state in which they'd found the property (uninhabited for seven years), and details of the life of the old woman who'd lived there have been provided by our neighbours. Madame Reynaud confined herself to one room (what is now the kitchen in the newer side) and still used the kitchen sink in the older side to wash her dishes. That was where the only cold tap was situated – the village had gone on to mains water (with meters) in the mid fifties.

As a novice builder *sans maître*, I developed my very own revolutionary pointing technique, using thick rubber gloves – I found a mortarboard too alien to handle – and a small mason's trowel! Scooping up a handful of cement in my gloved hand, I'd coax it into the scraped-out joints, push it in firmly and smooth it over with the trowel. It was slow but the only way I could control the cement! I didn't realise then that cement is not considered that precious and that it's quite in order to let some drop on the floor, but I couldn't bear the waste or the mess! Marcel, a French builder friend, when I described how I was working, laughed like a drain.

"Tu maçonnes comme une bijoutière!" (You're doing building work like a jeweller)

8

"Oui, mais le resultat me plaît; ça marche!" (Yeah, but I like the result; it works for me)

He visited one day when I was plastering in the downstairs, future lounge. I'd just one more bit to do, high up in a corner. He picked up the trowel loaded with cement and simply flicked it, spot on, into the right place!

"Il faut le faire comme ça!" (That's how you do it) I was duly humbled.

(On the whole, I think most of the males who visited the house, were somewhat surprised at what I was doing. This wasn't 'women's work' at all. But then, I've always enjoyed being unconventional!)

This room already had a flagstone floor, though it was uneven and cracked in places. Since some of the original plaster had refused to come off the walls, I'd roughly replastered three of them and painted them white, leaving a framework of stones visible around the doors and windows. The room badly needed lightening up anyway. The stones of the fourth wall, behind the chimneybreast were black, caked with soot – the job of cleaning them was awesome. I only went up to first floor level to start with, wirebrushing and washing them – a mammoth sandblasting treatment would have been required to clean them properly. They stayed dark, but once they were pointed with *chaux* (lime) cement, the contrast looked great. This place was going to be a bit different.

Over the years we made other improvements, beginning with basic plumbing and electrics[*]. An old butler sink came down with my parents from my London flat, when I updated my kitchen. It weighed a ton but they gamely transported it the 950-odd kilometers to Ribes! Alan got out his woodworking tools again and

---

[*] This was carried out by Daniel, who still lives in Ribes and does both. Always utterly charming when you rang him with a job or a problem, he'd say he'd be round. He wouldn't show up for a while and then unexpectedly he'd arrive, often with one or two others in tow, curious to see what we were doing to the place. I said to him jokingly once, "You know, Daniel, you're like English buses. You wait and wait and then three come at once!" I'm not sure he got it!

made a draining board and cupboard next to it. A geyser was installed over the sink and supplied hot water to the kitchen and to a shower and washbasin Daniel put in the bedroom above. From then on, Peg and Alan always complained that my shower worked better than theirs!

Our dear neighbours – part of the Balazuc family[*] – donated an old cooker and fridge when they were upgrading their kitchen. In the corner of the large upstairs mezzanine we installed a masticating toilet. Dédé had made us a beautiful new floor with the widest planks he had, some 15inches/39cms across, but in pine in the end; chestnut was too expensive. It was the biggest loo in the world, with just an old wooden screen to hide your modesty! This I found at an auction in Kent with sister-in-law Tina. It's covered with old postcards and cigarette cards dating from 1926 to 1934, and there's actually a postcard of the seafront at Westgate-on-Sea, where Peg and Alan were living. I think I paid £12 for it.

We finally had mod cons, but not that 'mod' actually! Because its use was so limited, the plumbing regulations, such as they were then, permitted the evacuation of the waste straight into the huge *puits perdu* (soakaway – this was the rubble-filled cellar of the demolished silk house, now the courtyard, into which all the waste water drains – a common practice in the countryside where there are no mains drains). Our bits and pieces of furniture, some of which are still in use, were on the basic side as well! We'd found an ancient metal bedframe hanging precariously through the rotten floor (that had to be replaced right in the beginning along with the roof). It's only 1.20m wide – an old-fashioned double. But, rubbed down and repainted and with a new mattress, it has served me – and now Mike too – very well for over thirty years. Narrow but very friendly!

On one early-on, exploratory visit to the dark nether regions of the old 'wing' (as we grandly called it at first!), Alan and I had dis-

---

[*] Geo Balazuc did most of the building work for my parents. His eldest son, Christian, married to Roberte, now lived – still do – in the house opposite, which belonged to Roberte's parents, Romain and Yvette Hernandez, also very dear friends of my parents. (See family tree, p90)

covered a large, worm-eaten pine chest. Its lid was completely rotten and we wrenched it off. It was so dark we could hardly see what was inside, but there was definitely something rather unsavoury in it from the smell. When we shone the torch on the interior, it was just a rotten old straw mattress full of dormouse nests! (We were later told that it had been a salt chest for storing the smoked ham products.) Treated and cleaned up and with a new lid made from the old chestnut floorboards, courtesy of Alan's carpentry skills, it was the second item of furniture in the new *'relooking'* (French for makeover!) of what came to be called 'Jan's side'. It also provided much-needed storage for linen and such.

Alan followed this commission up with a coffee table made from an old local brewery beer crate and more of those recycled chestnut planks. I'm sure he really enjoyed making these simple things; he liked working with wood. Peg passed over two single beds when she bought a new double for her guestroom, which gave us another sleeping space – with loo! – on the mezzanine. Downstairs, we added a few garden chairs and tables, and bingo, we had our second holiday home, one-star and only one up from camping, but what a thrill it was for us all! In the terrific heat of August, it's the coolest part of the property. Peg used to do an awful lot of cooking and entertaining for friends and visitors, and she was so pleased to have the extra space to offer and use herself.

I used to go down to Ribes whenever I could, sometimes just for a short holiday; on other occasions I'd leave a job just so that I could stay longer and do more work on 'my side'. Both sides of the property have typically small windows, which along with the one-metre thick walls help keep the place cool in summer and warm in winter. However, it does mean that, unless the sun's blazing outside, inside the light is extremely poor. One summer we decided we'd put in a second window, in the south-facing wall of what was now the kitchen. It was a relatively simple exercise, since there'd already once been a doorway there. This had originally led into the space used as a hen house, which my parents had also had demolished to increase the length of their terrace (see photo, page 87). The original lintel and door stones were vis-

11

ible and it was just a question of removing the fill-in stones to open up a space for a window. How big a window depended on what we could find.

We all three drove to the nearby village of Laurac to see the Tourel Brothers, the carpenters who'd made many of Peg and Alan's windows and shutters. Perhaps they'd have a window or two going spare! And what a stroke of luck! They had one in oak, which had been made to another customer's specification, but he hadn't come to collect or pay for it for over a year. It would fit the hole and it was ours – at a knockdown price. Now all I had to do was persuade Geo's second son, Alain, to help me install it. He was following in his father's footsteps and was learning the building trade. As it happened, he didn't need that much persuading. He was curious – the local guys always were – about the job, and the fact that I'd offered to help him, be his *manoeuvre* (mate or gofer). French women didn't tend to do this kind of thing. A couple of days later he turned up at the house.

"*Belle fenêtre.*" he said. "*En chêne?*" (Nice window. Oak?) "*C'était combien?*" (How much did you pay for it?) I told him the window's history.

He was obviously impressed by the price. "*Pas de problème pour l'installer.*" (No problem putting it in.)

"*Chouette, ça marche!*" I ran down the steps. "*Je fais du ciment toute de suite.*" (Great, I'll go and mix some cement.)

Two hours later, the window was installed and Alain had left for lunch. Peg and Alan came to admire.

"You're so jammy, Jan," said Peg. "I just don't know how you get them to do these things for you so quickly!"

"It's the gene mix," I said. "Father's charm, mother's sex appeal!"

We all had a drink to celebrate!

Another member of the Balazuc family, Geo's brother Serge, was involved in the next project – plastering the bedroom walls. 'Tonton' (Uncle) Serge is a real gem of a man; he seems to smile all the time. I haven't met many genuinely content people, but he seems to be. He's lived in the village all his life and has never left the Ardèche. He used to work with Geo, until a back injury limited the sort of work he could do. He'd helped with the extension of Peg and Alan's terrace and, after his accident, he continued to help them with light odd/gardening jobs (and still does the same for us). He's in his late sixties now, still dead good-looking (but has managed, chosen, to remain *célibataire*, unmarried). My father liked him enormously, impressed with his complete honesty, knowledge and wisdoms, and we have always trusted him utterly to keep an eye on things when we're not there. *"Je le fais comme si c'était chez moi,"* he'd always promise. (I'll look after it as if it were mine.)

That first working summer I'd removed all the old plaster from the bedroom walls and discovered underneath another doorway and several niches. These were again surrounded with beautiful, dressed stones, which I wanted to make features of as cubby-holes and shelves. The stones were also particularly fine in the first few courses above floor level and far too good to plaster over. We'd combine the two, then, I figured – pointed stones up to about 50cms all around the room as a kind of plinth, cum frieze, with plaster above, and the niche and doorway surround stones left exposed and pointed, as in the *salle de séjour* downstairs.

So, I got out the rubber gloves again and started pointing! Unfortunately, I was running out of time this visit and was hoping to leave the project for Serge to finish off with the help of some sketches with instructions of what to point, what to plaster. He was rather flabbergasted by the drawings – things just weren't done that way! – but he followed them to the letter and made a great job of it. Peg and Alan were extremely taken with the result.

"That was a really good idea," said Alan, who didn't give praise that lightly. "This could be the start of a whole new Ardechois style, you know! I do like the way all the rooms are different this side. Clever you!"

I glowed. "All that expensive design training didn't go to waste then." (I'd done an Interior Design course at Chelsea Art School in the early 1980s and they'd helped out financially.)

"Thanks, Al. Thanks to both of you."

The job satisfaction was incredible. We all felt we'd achieved a great deal. The house was very basic, but during the summer months, when so much time was spent outside, this simple accommodation was more than adequate, we thought. For years to come, friends and family were offered the dubious delights of staying in 'Jan's side'.

The last job that we all did together was to get the cement kitchen floor tiled. People who've read *Lilac and* Roses may remember that it was always something Peg had wanted their side, but by the time they were ready to do it, ceramic tiles would have cost too much – the poor exchange rate throughout the seventies did for them in the end. This time though the rate was better and we'd made a good contact through a friend who'd just had a swimming pool installed. The *carreleur* (tiler) did a really good and reasonably priced job for us, and I can still see Peg's delighted face when he'd finished.

One year I couldn't go to Ribes for work reasons and I will always regret it. 1990 was the year that Peg, aged 70, was diagnosed with melanoma. It started in France with a mole on her leg. She had it removed, but it came back. My parents hardly ever went to the doctor – they were part of that generation, who didn't "like to bother them" – unless they were really ill. Skin cancer did not have such a high profile then as now. She didn't seem to take it as seriously as she should have (in retrospect), or pass any concern for her health on to me or Ian. In fact, melanoma wasn't mentioned. None of us had any idea how quickly it could spread, but we would have nagged her to get herself treated – her French doctor had said he would get her into hospital in Montpellier straight away. But Alan was 80, poorly with emphysema, and Peg didn't want to leave him to look after himself. She said later she felt well, thought she was in no immediate danger and hadn't asked me to come down because she didn't want to "bother me". Instead, in early autumn, they came back to England and the National Health, where the wait for treatment was too long. The cancer spread everywhere and it was too late to save her. By February 1991 Peg was dead.

In the summers of the following two years, Alan and I spent time in Ribes in the company of two friends of my parents, Ron and Gerry. The first year I drove down to Ribes to get the house ready, and the three of them turned up a week later. Veronica (Ron) had worked for Alan at Surrey County Council Education Department. She and her husband had both already visited the house in previous years with their family, but I hadn't met them as yet. We all three now remember these as fairly happy holidays, even though Peg was so missed. Alan's breathing problems were worsening and this severely limited what he could do. But he was content to sit on the terrace, watching the house martins nest-building, and reading and reminiscing. He told a very good tale and enjoyed the audience[*].

We had a bit of a plumbing crisis the first year – the soil pipe in the courtyard was obviously leaking, as after every flush of the loo came that all too familiar smell of French drains. This time Daniel came promptly when we called. It was hard work digging the packed soil in the courtyard, as we followed the old cement pipe, to discover the culprit crack in a junction and roots completely blocking the flow of water. Daniel's 'repair' would defy an English plumber's belief, not to mention Council Building Control Officers – it certainly defied ours! We've often laughed in retrospect at the memory of it. He smashed a hole in the pipe, pulled out all the rogue roots and stuffed a smaller diameter plastic pipe inside the old one. He then wrapped several plastic carrier bags around the joins and covered the whole thing in *ciment prompt* (fast-setting cement).

"Bon, on prend un petit verre et ce sera prêt," he announced. (That'll be set by the time we've had a drink.)

On cue, I ran to get the cool beers. Quarter of an hour later he told me to flush the toilet and turn the taps on. We all waited with bated breath.

"Très bien. Ça coule. (It's flowing) *C'est fini."* Plumbing problem sorted, Ardèche-style!

---

[*] Ron and Gerry, after hearing Alan talking about a book on cricket that he'd written and had had published, while at SCC, under the pseudonym of Christopher Sly, *How To Bowl Them Out*, set about finding a copy, as he hadn't kept one. It took them about six months and Alan was tickled pink when he got it. They've since found two other copies!

One day of the last holiday will stay in all of our minds, too; it was such a happy one. It was mid June and Gerry's birthday. Blue skies and glorious sunshine greeted us on rising – it happens a lot in Ribes, I have to say! I busied myself with breakfast – Bucks Fizz for starters – and put *The Beatles' White Album* on the hi-fi, turning up the volume when Paul starts screaming "Today is your birthday; happy birthday to you."

"Rise and shine like the sun! Breakfast's ready," I called out. Squeals of delight from Ron as she and Gerry came out onto the terrace.

"Hiya, Ron. Hi, Gerry, birthday boy!" I pressed champagne flutes into their hands.

"Cheers, mate, hope it'll be a goody. Sit down and enjoy."

Alan appeared. I gave him a hug, made sure he was settled and went off to see to scrambled eggs with smoked salmon on toast, warm the *croissants* and make coffee. What a feast! We lingered a while after finishing all these *délices*, but by eleven we had to move, the sun was getting too hot. Besides, we were all invited to lunch at some American friends of Peg and Alan and would shortly have to be on our way to arrive soon after midday – sacred eating time in France in those days (though things are changing a bit now).

Then, a very pregnant Min appeared on the scene. She was a local feral cat, but had been a friend of ours for some time. She loved the garden and spent a great deal of time there, alternately hunting and sleeping. She seemed more than pleased to see us and rubbed her fat, tortoiseshell body against all our legs.

"I think her kittens are due any time," said Ron, gently feeling her tummy. "Can you hang on 'til we're back this afternoon, Min?"

We all went off to get ready to go out, but just as we were about to get into the car, Ron, who'd been strolling round the garden, shouted out:

"Min's having her kittens! Oh, quick, come and look!"

Gerry and I ran up the steps to the mimosa tree under which Min had installed herself to give birth. Alan, unfortunately, wasn't up to this.

"Al, can you find her a box and an old dustsheet or something in the cellar," I asked over my shoulder.

There she lay, along with one very tiny and bloody black kitten, extremely new to the world and ignored by mum, who was more than occupied with the others on their way. The three of us stood and watched, entranced.

"How many, I wonder. We've got to stay and see this," I said. "I'll go get a camera and call Cecile and explain we'll be a bit delayed!"

By midday, Min had had five kittens, all in different permutations of her black, white and tan colours. We left them the box with its bedding nearby, but we had to tear ourselves away.

Cecile and Harold live in an idyllic location – a huge, stone house, complete with tower and circular stone staircase, high above the town of Les Vans, and a large terrace looking out over the magnificent mountain scenery which surrounds the Chassezac river valley. They retired there from the States – Cecile is half French – and the house was originally the family home, which they had managed to reacquire. Like most Americans, they are amazingly friendly and hospitable and they were waiting for us round the shaded dining table on the terrace, Harold with cocktail shaker poised and Cecile keeping an anxious eye on what was happening in the kitchen – she's a brilliant cook.

French lunches are a real challenge – four hours eating minimum, different wines with every course, and today, of course, more champagne with the birthday cake dessert around 5pm! We could barely move and needed several cups of Harold's "kawffee" before making our farewells and our contented way home. No sign of Min or kittens, so we all collapsed on our terrace, recovering from the emotions and pleasures of the day and watching first the housemartins then the bats wheeling around in the gathering dusk. Min finally put in an appearance, one of the tiny bundles in her mouth, and laid it proudly at our feet for our inspection. After we'd all praised and cooed, she picked it up and headed off to the cellar. At around nine Alan went off to bed, and the three of us stayed on the terrace, revelling in the peace. The millions of stars were starting to appear in the night sky, together with a newish moon, and we were all feeling tired but extremely happy and at one with the world.

"You know, Jan," Gerry said, "you'll probably find this pretty funny. Just before we got here, Alan said to me: 'Look, Gerry, don't take this personally, but I don't think Jan will like you. She has an extremely low opinion of men.'"

"What!" I guffawed, remembering back to their arrival. I'd been sitting chatting with the neighbours opposite on their terrace, had come leaping down their steps, all smiles and hugs, and we'd proceeded to get on extremely well!

"Al seems to have got you all wrong then?" Gerry suggested.

"Dear Al," I sighed. "I don't think he really understands me at all. I prefer male company, as he does. It's just when I have relationships with men that they usually end up disappointing me. For starters, I haven't met a man yet who didn't think that his time – and therefore his life – was more important than mine."

Little did I know that very soon I was to meet a man who wasn't like that, who wouldn't disappoint me, just keep on impressing me!

- 2 -
UP ON THE ROOF

IT'S MY FIRM belief that it was always my parents', certainly my mum's, assumption and hope that La Clède would stay in the family – she wanted us to be Europeans. My brother, his wife Tina and their children, Tom and Molly, had all visited over the years. They'd been living in Singapore and Kuala Lumpur, where Ian was working for the British Council, running English language schools, and had had one or two holidays in Ribes while the kids were still very young. They returned to the UK when Tom and Molly needed to start formal education.

I was single, living in north London, frequently changing jobs, as I found less and less satisfaction with most of the architectural practices I was employed by. Besides, it gave me the chance to travel, and visit my parents in France – I've never been very happy with only four weeks' holiday a year! Without family commitments, I had a great deal of flexibility to do more of what I wanted to do in my life. Alan and I had discussed the possibility of letting the house after our last visit to Ribes together.

"It's the only way to pay all the overheads," I said. "I've done some research. We could get at least three hundred quid a week in high season, no problem. Even if we just let eight to ten weeks, we'll be covered."

Alan looked surprised at the price I'd quoted.

"Good heavens! Is that right? I'd no idea." He mused for a moment or two.

"Well, it's certainly a very pleasant and comfortable house, but the Ardèche is nowhere near as busy as other areas. You know, most people we talk to haven't even heard of it! How are you going to advertise it?"

I'd done my research. "I've found an organisation that brings out a brochure every year, where the owners, mostly English, advertise their French holiday homes – there's about a thousand in this year's." Alan's eyes widened.

"The brochure's advertised in the broadsheet press; interested people phone for a copy and get in touch with the owners direct. We do the admin and take all the rent. The brochure's just a shop window. We'll have to do our own literature, of course."

"The place hasn't been touched for years," said Alan, showing some doubt finally.

"I know, it'll need a bit of a facelift. But I can decorate it gradually. All the basics are there already. And it's got a lovely homey feel to it. In fact, it's not basic at all – washing machine, dishwasher. We can leave the stereo and the TV and all the books. Most *gîtes* are pretty bare, apparently."

"Well, it's worth a try certainly. You'll be there all the time, will you?" asked Alan.

"Absolutely, yes. I think I'll have to be, in case anything goes wrong. Terrible job, but someone's got to do it!"

I busied myself compiling a little brochure and all the other necessary paperwork. The timing seemed perfect – the deadline for the ad was the end of September. The brochure came out in November for the following season 1994, so my literature had to be ready by then. Fortunately, my current job at City University provided a computer and access to the printing department.

My first holiday 'season' began in early June 1994. I was still grieving for Peg, and now Alan, dead only a few months. After Peg's death in '91 I took her ashes to Ribes. I got Cecile and Harold and Serge together at the house one late afternoon. My parents' American friends wanted to buy something for Peg's garden in her memory. I suggested a *lagerstroemia*, a mediterranean shrub/tree, which blooms in August when we're a bit short on colour because of the heat. We planted it and the ashes in what became Peg's Bed at the side of the rear terrace. And together we all – even Serge who hardly ever drinks – drank a glass of champagne to her. In '94, I brought Alan's ashes too and scattered them under his tree. This time my good friend Glynis[*] and friends of my parents, Michael and Margaret, joined me in a similar ceremony. Some fifteen years previously, Alan had stuck a conker in the ground just to see if it would grow. When it did, he said he hoped he'd live long enough to sit in its shade. He did, and his beautiful chestnut shades us whenever we get the chance to lounge in the hammock (which isn't often, let me tell you!)

That first letting year, I was totally paranoid most of the time, convinced that appliances, plumbing and electrics were all going to go haywire, that guests would break things, even steal. But I put on my PR face and, when I couldn't solve anything myself, I always had my helpful neighbours and friends. I wasn't often lonesome, spending day after day pottering about in the garden. I was never happier than when doing this, and it has become a passion. Apart from my obvious chores, cleaning and washing linen on changeoever day, it was absolute bliss to be timeless with no deadlines or pressures. Only the church clock marked the time, ringing – like most churches in the south – once on the half hour and twice every hour[**] (plus three masses a day).

On the whole, the letting went surprisingly successfully and most of the guests were lovely. At the end of the first year, I thought: I can handle this, two lives – six months' town living in the UK, six months' country living in France – best of both worlds. Downshifting certainly suited me. I was my own boss – at last. This was definitely for me!

You may well be asking at this point: "What about the brother? Didn't he have any say in all of this?"[***] Here I have to confess: very little. I more or less presented him and Tina with a *fait accompli*. We did have words, but came to an amicable arrangement in the end. They've forgiven me now, I think, and they still visit, but they've never been as passionate about the place as I have. They have their own lives and their own rural retreat in Shropshire.

---

[*] Glynis helped me out with the lets during my first year and was my UK rep, for which many thanks.

[**] People ask why this happens. It's simply in case you didn't hear or count first time, when you were a peasant labouring in the fields with no personal timepiece!

[***] We both knew from the *notaire* that in the long term, since I have no children, Tom and Molly would inherit it.

I'd sold my London flat during the year. When I returned to England in the autumn, there was Alan's flat in Kent to sell and a new home for myself to buy and do up, to let during my summer season in France. (I planned to live on rents – a property tart!) It was quite an onerous action list, particularly as I wasn't entirely sure where I wanted to live. Most of my friends were in north London and north of it, but was it a good idea to move further away from southern France – or better still, closer to it? My final choice was Canterbury, only half an hour from Dover and the continent, and with "an extremely buoyant letting market" I was told by agents. I fell in love with the first house I saw, but looked at all the others anyway. Nothing compared. It was two tiny cottages knocked into one, end of terrace (of five houses), right next to the river (Great Stour), located on the site of the old city wall and five minutes' walk to the high street. But it was old (1857), in a conservation area and needed a lot of work, according to my surveyor.

Katy, the daughter of one of my close friends Ce(lia), was in the final year of her Art and Film degree at Christchurch College, and I spent good times with her and her friends both on campus and around the city. Canterbury had a very youthful feel to it with so many students around – Kent University is also based there – and plenty of interesting specialist shops and hang-outs, as well as the magnificent cathedral and olde worlde buildings. But there wasn't much time for leisure pursuits. I had nine weeks to complete the works schedule and let the house!

Things were certainly changing in my life in 1995 and more was to come. In April, I met Michael James Kay. I didn't even have to advertise – he turned up at my door! I was still based in my dad's flat in Birchington while it was in the process of being sold. It was half an hour away from Canterbury by car, and I drove to my 'building site' every day to oversee and help out with the work. One of the major jobs in progress was a new damp course. I'd got a couple of quotes from organisations in the Yellow Pages, but I wasn't happy with them. The vendors of the house recommended someone they'd used in the past, and Mike arrived as part of this outfit, to make good after all the destruction. We both often go cold at the thought of how this might just not have happened, and how so much of what occurs in life is pure chance – or fate, depending on your point of view. It was a good atmosphere in the house – I was high on it all; having a team of blokes around doing just what you want is a real buzz! There was a lot of banter and gentle flirting, but Mike says it was the list in the tea/coffee-making area of who had milk and sugar, how much, and the excellent biscuits that won him over in the beginning! I admit I had an ulterior motive in being charming to them all. We had to work fast, and I also needed to find an English builder to mend 'my' roof in France, which had been leaking for several years[*]. I'd asked for several estimates from French builders the year before, but they seemed astronomical, taking into account a dreadful exchange rate of around seven francs to the pound. This can make a real difference when you're spending thousands. I quickly discovered that there wasn't much that fazed Mike when it came to buildings. I learned that throughout the eighties he'd purchased, renovated and resold nineteen houses!

"Ever done any roofs?" I lightly dropped into the conversation one day.

"No, I don't do roofs," he said. "Can't stand heights."

My heart sank. "Do you, by any chance, know a man who does?"

"Yes, but, if this is for your French house, he won't go to France to do it."

"Oh." (One more try, I thought!) "Well, my roof couldn't be simpler really. It's just timbers with pantiles resting on top. Just needs some new tiles, a bit of sealing round the edges and some insulation and boarding inside. How d'you fancy coming down for a free holiday to check it out? My neighbour's a retired builder; he can lend scaffolding and such, and materials aren't a problem; there are big stores like B&Q these days."

---

[*] This was the roof that Peg had had redone back in 1965. It had been a very basic job, using old tiles and not much else, since it wasn't to be the side that would be lived in at first. The leaks weren't that noticeable, especially in summer when it hardly rained, but obviously it wasn't good for the house and needed to be done.

I could tell he wasn't dismissing the idea out of hand and I guessed he liked a challenge. I also knew he was a Capricorn and very determined.

"I'll think about it," he promised.

And down to Ribes he came in July. We looked at lots of other Ardechois roofs as well as La Clède's, visited builders' merchants, discussed methods. I wined and dined him, promised him beautiful weather right into autumn, desperately hoping that he'd take it on.

"I can do this," he said at last. "How about October?"

It was teeming with rain – hadn't stopped for two days. Seven-thirty in the evening and I was waiting in the *gîte* kitchen for Mike and his two fellow workers, Malcolm and Kieran, to arrive. The table was set for four and baked potatoes and a lamb casserole were in the oven. I'd emptied the old side of the house and had had the timbers treated (those Tourel brothers again). I'd borrowed scaffolding and a cement mixer from Geo; the tiles were stacked on pallets in the courtyard. An English friend, another Michael, who lived nearby, had left his trailer – he was going to take away all the hardcore for his drive. All was ready. The phone rang.

"Hi, Jan, it's Mike. We're in Le Puy. How much further?"

"Oh dear, Mike, it's at least another two hours from there!"

He groaned. "Sod it. I thought we were closer than that. This weather's dreadful. Hasn't stopped raining all the way down. Thought you said …"

"I know, it's pissing down here as well, but it will stop soon. It never lasts more than three days."

"Oh well, we'd better get on. Malcolm can drive for a bit."

"Do be careful coming down the mountain pass, especially in the dark. It's the hardest bit and always at the end of the journey when you're tired. But there's a hot meal waiting. See you around ten. Take care, won't you."

Two and a half hours later, I heard the van. I grabbed umbrellas and ran down the steps into the courtyard, streaming with water. The rain was still very heavy. The van was parked at the foot of the narrow entrance ramp, the driver, Malcolm, I assumed, uncertain whether it would make it up.

"Hello, you poor things," I called out. "Leave the van there for now. It won't be blocking anybody."

Three very weary guys got out of the enormous Victoria Hire van. I handed them open umbrellas.

"Hi, there. Just follow me up. Who fancies a beer for starters?"

Back in the kitchen, I shook them all by the hand. "This weather's a terrible welcome. Sorry about it. Toilet's just through there. We'll have a drink and some food. Then you can all just crash. You must be knackered."

An hour later, it was obvious they all felt much better. They'd consumed ten beers, the huge casserole, which I'd naively thought would do for two meals, a large salad and three *baguettes*. I'd prepared and frozen several meals, but I hadn't reckoned on these appetites! Much more cooking would be required. I showed them all their bedrooms. Kieran, the youngest at nineteen and the gofer in the team, elected to fall into his bed straight away. Malcolm decided to have one more beer and one more roll-up and then do likewise.

"Any idea on the weather forecast?" Mike asked me.

"Same again tomorrow, apparently," I said gloomily. "Perhaps there's stuff we can do inside. Anyway, don't think about it tonight. You all need a good night's sleep now, more than anything else. Off you go. I'll clear this lot." Malcolm headed off upstairs.

"I'll give you a hand first," said Mike, jumping to his feet and impressing me again.

"Thanks, Mike, but go get some sleep. The dishwasher'll do it. I just hope it doesn't keep you awake. The model's called a Silence, but it doesn't half make a row!"

It was still raining the next day. When it rains in the Ardèche, it really rains. With the village built on a mountainside, every road and path becomes a river and every flight of steps a rushing cascade of rainwater. Mike, having checked out all the leaks, now clearly visible, spent most of the time disconsolately looking out of the windows at the leaden skies, impatient to start, and thinking a lot. The other two played cards – they soon tired of the TV in a foreign language. The *météo* was pessimistic. I went shopping for more food.

The following day there was a short break, which coincided with the arrival of Marc, the baker, doing his round. I ran down to his van to replenish the fresh bread stocks, while telling him of our predicament and asking him about his forecast. He always knows about the weather and nine times out of ten he's right.

"Demain il fera beau," he announced with confidence. *"Tu peux commencer ton chantier."* (You'll be able to start your job tomorrow.)

"Right then," said Mike, "if Marc says it'll be fine tomorrow, we'll put the scaffolding up today in the rain. We Brits are used to it. C'mon, you two. Get your waterproofs on!"

Marc was right! As so often happens in this part of the country, we awoke next day to clear blue skies and blazing sunshine. By midday, everything was dry again and it was impossible to imagine the previous downpour. This is why the locals are never too concerned about leaks. The damp simply doesn't linger like it does in Britain. If you mention leaks, they typically shrug shoulders. *"Ça séchera,"* they say philosophically. (It'll dry.) And it always does.

The entire job took sixteen days and we were blessed with fine weather throughout. At times, it certainly was a challenge. Nothing Is Easy, and I mean nothing, with these old houses, built with very crude, irregular timbers; no wall is straight, no corner a right angle. Some days it was so hot it was impossible to work on the roof between noon and three. There was a big headache with the new pantiles being too narrow for the old rafters. Mike, king of improvisation, solved the problem, solved every problem, rose to every occasion. He never mentioned how he was feeling working at high level, just concentrated on the job in hand.

Malcolm was a stalwart ally. He was retired and had just completed the building of his own house, so he was a jack-of-all trades as well. They'd met when he frequented Mike's café in Whitstable. They reminisced and gossiped, swapping job-solving ideas around as they worked, stopping only to cry out: "Another bucket of muck, Kieran! Get a move on!" The one and only time Mike got upset was when he looked down from the roof to see Kieran sprawled out in a deckchair, soaking up the sun when he was supposed to be mixing cement. He came storming down the ladder with an empty bucket, which he threw to the ground in a rage.

"More bloody muck, Kieran. Don't do this again please!"

He was a fantastic team leader, not a hard taskmaster. He certainly believed people should work for their money. But no-one worked harder than Mike. I've never seen such productivity. (It's been that way throughout his working life from all the tales he's told me of all the careers he's had. And I thought I'd had a varied life!) Even when the rest of us were 'finished' for the day, he'd still be at it, always planning and catering for what lay ahead. In 1995, Mike was 58 and Malcolm was 62. Christian, our neighbour, 43, would call out how impressed he was with these two foreign old-timers grafting away opposite.

"C'est impressionant!" he'd shout. "Que vous avez la forme, messieurs!" (How fit you are!)

We had time off too, of course. The countryside around us is stunning, with range after range of mountains visible from the village. The higher you go, the better the views get! There are small, remote hamlets all over the mountains, very close as the crow flies, but many kilometres of twisting river roads and hairpin bends to reach them. The roads are extremely narrow, very often with sheer drops at the sides. Riding at the back of a car, you can be inclined to feel somewhat queasy. I was driving my trusty Renault 5, with Mike beside me, Malcolm and Kieran behind, and we were doing a tour of the beautifully wild Drobie river valley up on to the Cévennes Corniche, which has just phenomenal views in every direction. Every so often I'd look in the rear-view mirror to check on reactions. Kieran, typically, was in "seen one mountain, seen 'em all" mode. Malcolm's eyes stared ahead constantly, his hands tightly gripping the seat.

"Thank God I drove down these roads in the dark," I heard him mutter to himself!

How hard we all worked – sometimes ten or twelve hours a day. We played, too, lots of games – cards, Monopoly, Scrabble, the lot. We were usually too tired to go out, but it has to be said that there wasn't much going on in out-of-season Joyeuse, or even Aubenas, our equivalent of "The Big Smoke." No-one else spoke French, so we had to amuse ourselves. Board games aren't really my thing, but they can be very bonding and quite a laugh after a heavy physical day. Everyone ate very well – they seemed to like my cooking, thankfully, as it's far from English. Both my brother and I had a great cookery teacher in Peg – she was adamant about treating us equally, regardless of gender roles – as she was taught by a French woman, Géllo, whose family she stayed with, aged eighteen, as *au pair* to her daughter Monique. That's when her love affair with France began.

Goodness knows how Peg did it, with no car and a full-time teaching job, but she put home-made, three-course meals (plus cheese if we wanted) on the table for four every night for years. Now, that was pretty hard work. No supermarkets around then. How many contemporary working wives would contemplate that? My sister-in-law Tina is one, aided by Ian. She's mentioned to me how sulky Tom and Molly had been when told they had to sit and eat proper meals together *en famille*, instead of microwaved, prepared stuff in their rooms, like most of their peers. Eight years or so down the line, the kids both like cooking and have thanked their parents for enforcing this. I know they also had Jamie Oliver as a role model, but who says firmness doesn't pay off?

Mike had estimated two and a half weeks for the whole job, so we had less pressure once the roof was completed ahead of schedule. We had a convenient storm soon after, which provided an opportunity to test it. Mike and I had been invited by some French neighbours to go for a drink that day to celebrate. Mike and Malcolm had been finishing off the new ceiling inside, while outside it was raining buckets – *à seau* – again.

"Oh shit!" There was a loud exclamation. Malcolm had just pointed out to Mike two trickles of water from the join with the ceiling above the chimneybreast.

"I don't believe it. "Where's that coming from?"

Mike groaned. "Damn. Well, we can't check it now. We'll have to wait until it stops. Tomorrow."

Mike was clearly extremely frustrated and fed up that he could do nothing. It was a real downer – our first big setback. We were too dejected to go out and I had to ring to apologise, which, as it was already well past six, didn't go down well. When you have a formal invitation from the French, they normally go to a lot of trouble to choose some fine wine and prepare lots of delicious nibbles – *amuse-gueules* – to go with, which they'd probably already done. But socialising was beyond us. (We went the following evening, had all the treats from the day before, plus champagne, and had a great time, despite Mike's meagre French.) First thing the next day, the two men had been back on high, checking and reinforcing the concrete fillet, which joined the roof to the party wall in the apex of the two houses.

I'll have to return to the subject of this 'damn' wall again. We finally 'solved' the leak problem years later in 2002. It's been a real headache ever since the neighbouring house was heightened an extra floor in 1969. (There's a photo of it being done in *Lilac and Roses* and you can see the difference between new and old wall in the photograph at the beginning of this book.) It was extremely poorly and cheaply built at the time by the previous neighbour, Monsieur Mettayer. In fact, it should never have been extended – upwards or sideways, so that his bathroom window was a mere half metre away from one of ours! (In summer, when our window on that north side is open to cool the house, we know exactly when our new neighbours brush their teeth and use the toilet! Nice.)

In the sixties, no planning permission was necessary, and people just did what they wanted, usually with as few outgoings as possible, as they always had. Peg and Alan had bitten their tongues and kept quiet about it, to be diplomatic – since they were outsiders and only there in summer – except when it leaked into their side of the house as well, into their bedroom. Mr Mettayer then did a patch-up job and at least it stopped that leak. Aesthetically, the extension's certainly no improvement to the way **our** property now looks from our side, and we have always had leaks when it rains heavily.

Because we had some spare time, Mike and Malcolm very kindly said they would do a few odd jobs that were crying out for attention, one of which was Daniel's plastic bag plumbing repair described earlier (though, to give him his due, it had lasted!) Malcolm's face, when he saw it, was an utter picture! As an ex-plumber and water board inspector, he'd come across some things in his working life. I think this was the peachiest. We'd see him chuckling to himself thereafter, as he rolled one of his mini-cig-gies, and we knew he was reliving it! One of those stories to be recalled over many a pint, I'm sure. In its place, the dear man insisted on installing a sophisticated, three-way cement junction in a proper *regard* (inspection manhole), greatly to facilitate future plumbing checks. This has proved to be a godsend and I will be eternally grateful to him.

All through the work, our surrounding neighbours kept a curi-ous eye on progress and methods, offering, as often as not, their bits of advice. We'd wave and chat to them from the roof. One of the French estimates had come from the then *maire*, Monsieur Barbut, a well-respected builder (and an extremely honest mayor by all accounts). I'd felt obliged to write to him explaining that, with the current exchange rate, the cost was too much and that, just this once, for such a large job, I'd asked an English team to come and do it. I could only afford for it to be done in the tradi-tional, simple way. With old tiles on top of new, the end result would not be much changed.

Vital diplomacy, I felt. I was recalling accounts of the bad feel-ing and graffiti, which appeared locally towards the end of the sixties, following the start of the Dutch invasion of the Ardèche. Most of them apparently bought nothing here, bringing every-thing they needed with them. The Belgians are also omnipresent in the area and do the same. But things have changed these days. All nationalities mostly now shop at the supermarkets and DIY chainstores, which didn't exist before. In our local *Champion*, most products are now labelled in Flemish as well as French.

On the evening before "The Roofers of Ribes" were due to leave and return to Kent, Mike wanted us all to go out for a meal together to celebrate what had been a pretty successful operation, bar the minor leak. (It hadn't rained again to test the extra work to the roof fillet.) We booked a table at the Hôtel de l'Europe in Joyeuse. While we were waiting for our orders, Mike told us all the tale of his last visit to France in 1985. He and his family had been staying at a friend's place in Rosas, just the other side of the French/Spanish border. On the return drive back through France, they'd been shunned, refused petrol, food and shelter again and again at the hands of the French. Unknown to them, there'd been a disaster at the Heysel football stadium in Belgium, leading to the deaths of 39 fans and English supporters had been blamed. (It led to a five-year blanket ban on English clubs in European football.) Mike, unaware of the news, couldn't understand what was going on, but he was very sure, once he'd finally got them all on the ferry, that he would never go back to "That Country".

We were all amazed to hear about the treatment he'd received. I'd never heard such a tale about the French, never had such a bad experience.

"It took a great deal to get me to come back," he said, looking directly at me. I blushed.

"But I have to say, I love this countryside. The people are charming. The village and the house are brilliant. And the weather … It's certainly balanced things up a bit as far as I'm concerned!"

"Well," I said, "you've certainly impressed the French – and me, I hasten to add. You're welcome back any time."

- 3 -
WHITE KNIGHT IN A WHITE VAN (1997)

BUT IT WASN'T until 1997 that Mike and I were both together again in Ribes. The previous year was not a good one for him. His twenty-eight year marriage had come to grief and he had left the family home. His two daughters, Louise and Clare, had already left to go to university, and Clare was in her final year of a nursing degree in Hatfield. Louise had also done a BSc – in podiatry – and was practising in Gloucester with her partner, Lawrence, who was a podiatrist too (foot doctor, for those unfamiliar with the term). Mike was living, not very comfortably, in a pretty basic flat above a friend's army surplus shop. We quickly realised we were both unhappy apart and passed many an hour monopolising the phone lines between Canterbury and Ribes. During the winter of '96/97 in Canterbury we spent a lot of time together, though it had to be somewhat clandestine, for fear of rocking any boats.

That spring, when I drove to France in my faithful Renault 5 to open up the house for another season, Mike came with me, intending to return a couple of weeks later to Canterbury. (He needed to sort out his affairs and buy and renovate a house for himself.) Delighting in the freedoms Ribes offered and living together for the first time *à la française*, we were getting more and more involved, hardly believing how happy we were in each other's company. I'd spent so many years living on my own; now we seemed inseparable. I knew it wouldn't take much to convince me that I had finally found my soulmate, and the moment soon arrived. I'd discovered a lump in my right breast and arranged to have a mammogram at a clinic in Aubenas. Mike came with me.

I was driving, the traffic was terrible and the appointment time was getting closer. Stuck in a jam not far from the clinic, I jumped out.

32

"I'll have to walk from here, Mike. Will you park the car? There's a free car park just up there," I indicated. "The clinic's down this road. I'll meet you back here in about an hour, OK?" I rushed off, abandoning him to a strange town and the honking cars behind. About fifty minutes later, I left the clinic and saw Mike coming towards me with such a look of concern on his face.

"It's all right," I called out, as he approached. "It's only a cyst after all. They've drained it and it'll be fine."

"Oh, Jan." He rushed into my arms and held me like I'd never been held before, kissing me all over my face, tears falling from us both. Passers-by looked and smiled, but we were only into each other.

"I was so worried about you," he said between kisses. "But how come you got a result so quickly?"

"It's different here," I said, laughing with relief and the high I was on. I kissed him back. This man was extraordinary. I couldn't fault him, didn't have to worry that he couldn't cope. He could. He was bright, strong, sincere, capable, dependable ... and pretty nice-looking **and** a groovy dresser, too. And he fixed things.

"You're amazing," I beamed. "I Think I Love You."

"I Wanna Be Your Man," he counteracted. I pulled him close to me.

"You're on," I said.

We walked arm in arm back to the car. The car park has a wonderful view overlooking the Ardèche river and the Drôme mountains fading away into the distance. We gazed at them; we gazed at each other. We weren't really there, but we were.

"I'm so happy to be here with you, sharing life with you. I can't believe it's happening sometimes." I kissed him.

"Let's have a coffee," Mike suggested, "and calm down a bit before we drive back!"

Later that week, we had a sad and tearful parting at Valence bus station. Mike was driven off in a coach, with its two weary drivers on their long run from southern Spain to England, and I drove home in the dark to an empty house in Ribes, and to new *locataires* (paying guests) arriving the next day. There was the comfort and therapy of my garden, but I was feeling very lonely indeed and already missed him desperately.

I was out there as usual one morning in early July, on the first garden terrace, pruning (one of my favourite garden jobs), when I heard a vehicle approaching. I looked up and, to my utter disbelief, saw Mike's white Bedford van driving up the ramp into the courtyard.

"Mike," I screamed. "What are you doing here?"

I rushed down to greet and hug him. Separated from me once again, he'd decided on impulse to come down for my birthday. He'd postponed a client's job and had just set off one evening after work, filling the van with bits and pieces of furniture I'd stored with him, together with silly prezzies and things he knew I'd like.

"Hello, darling," he grinned. "I Drove All Night to get to you."

"That's a great song title," I joked, hugging him some more. "I can't think of one, I'm all in a tizz! You lovely man, how fantastic to see you. You must be exhausted."

"I just had to make sure I'd done the right thing, so we can all move forward. I want this new life with you, Jan. D'you know, it was only when I turned up the road to Ribes that I said to myself 'What on earth do I do if Jan's not there?' Hardly know anyone, don't speak the lingo." He smiled, but he didn't care now. I didn't care. He was here again. We both knew he'd have managed fine, of course, but I'm extremely glad to say I **was** there to greet him!

We were so lucky, the *gîte* was free that week. No guests, so the place was ours. No chores or duties, just lots of fun and outings and spoiling ourselves. The time flew by and Mike suddenly had to be on his way back again. But this time our separation wouldn't be for too long. He'd made an offer on an old terraced cottage in Canterbury – on the city wall, like mine, but on the south side. The same woman had been living there since the forties and there was absolutely nothing modern about it and an awful lot that was rotten! The whole house would have to be gutted for new wiring and plumbing, central heating, new roof – the works. Nothing to a veteran like Mike, who'd been in this position a few times before! I said I'd drive back to the UK if his offer was accepted and help him work on it, leaving La Clède and guests in the hands of a friend and her husband, who'd visited several times and had offered to mind things for me – us. I had to get used to the plural now.

Mike had taken a cab and was waiting for me at Dover with a big bunch of flowers and A Whole Lotta Love. After emotional tears and much nose-blowing, we drove to Canterbury, talking twenty to the dozen, in a state of intoxication and itching to get our hands on each other some more. Mike, ever sensitive, had organised a secret location – my house was let, of course – in an attempt not to upset anyone who might see us. He's lived and worked in the area for over twenty years and knows a lot of people. This was a friend's student house, which was empty and being decorated while the students were on vacation. 'Our' room was full of flowers and candles – I just couldn't believe I'd won the heart of this wonderful man ... I'd never been so romanced, so consistently!

We've been together ever since, and when I say together, I mean together, like joined at the hip! We barely spend any time apart. However, as I write this now in June 2003, we are apart for the first time since then, and for a longish period – sixteen days to be precise. Mike left to go to Oxford where daughter Clare has bought her first flat. We both saw it before we left this year, and it was an utter tip of a place, although we could all see its potential. It had character, unlike all of the other properties she'd looked at in the same price bracket – it just needed Mike's magic touch. We had hoped to do the work together before we left for France. We work well and fast, and 'changing rooms' (and houses) is our speciality. But the purchase had dragged on, as they do, while reports and surveys were carried out, and we had to be in France (oh dear!) to get the house and garden ready for this year's guests. Mike had promised his help, though, and he had to go and do what a dad has to do, as he does everything he does – with organisation, practicality, patience, skill and love.

But we were in limbo, not knowing his precise departure date, dependent on completion day and the handing over of keys. And it was hot – *la canicule*, they call it – August weather two months early. I was on edge, about his leaving and the heat. As usual, he was thinking ahead, calmly planning. Not a word from him about any emotional upset **he** was going through. While I whinged, he kept himself busy.

Géo's son, Christian is our neighbour opposite. He has the odd combination of skinhead hairdo and enormous walrus moustache and works to live, or rather, he bank manages to hunt – his main passion in life. He's having a new house built higher up our mountain. That is, what he can't do himself or with the help of his brothers and mates. It's almost at the top and the view is to die for – one hundred and eighty degrees of mountain range after mountain range, getting hazier and more magical with the distance; it looks beautiful whatever the weather. It's the most wonderful site. He had intended this house to be a *gîte*. However, rather foolishly, he admits himself now, one night in a *moment de bonne humeur*, he told his daughter, Orane, and her current *mec* (fella) that they could live there. This affair is now over, but he promised – "*Je suis pendu*" (I can't get out of it), he said, as he came home late from site one night looking exhausted. This was after a day's banking, feeding his troop of hunting dogs and retrieving one that had got away, and then a good few hours of building work of some kind. The things some dads do for their daughters!

Mike had offered to help him lay laminate flooring on the first floor. This offer of help is an ongoing thing with Mike, not only because he's endlessly generous anyway, but because he feels so lacking in the French language department, though he's really making progress – everyone says so. He wants to give in another way, in the language he speaks, which is *bricolage* – building, creating, repairing, fixing – call it what you will. He also needs to get away from me sometimes and into some serious male bonding. (I remember some English male comedian/personality – but not who – in a radio interview last winter saying, "Every man should have a shed!" Mike has two sheds in Canterbury and three cellar rooms here – Christian borrows the fourth for his building stuff – and the van, too, of course.) As far as talking French goes, he has a growing vocabulary, with not much grammar, but he's not afraid, like so many foreigners, to jump in and, if he can't say something, act it out. (Christian understands a lot more English than he lets on, anyway.) And if I'm not there doing the talking, *il doit se débrouiller* (he has to manage). So, it's very good for him (and I've joked with him that, as a Capricorn, he needs constant challenges. I must be right; he puts up with me!)

Thus, they communicated and worked together for the two days it took. And apparently had a lot of laughs and *moments agréables*, with mock arguments about who really was *le chef* (boss) and who should make the decisions. Brothers and neighbours dropped in to watch and admire. They love to look into Mike's van, which is an Aladdin's cave, full of tools and gadgets, like a workshop on wheels, and so well organised, with all his bits and pieces in labelled containers on racks. Apart from his other talents, he's a born archivist[*].

"Qu'est-ce qu'on a bossé," said Christian to me afterwards, as he and Roberte came over to our terrace with a thank-you five-litre *bidon* of Gamay. (Have we ever worked!)

"C'est un homme exceptionnel que tu as; tu dois le garder." (That's a great guy you've got there; you wanna hold on to him.) He hugged me and said thank you for the loan. Mike had loved the whole experience – the usual job satisfaction, everyone's delight at the end result, getting to know the Balazucs better.

"Plus, I'm becoming bilingual," he said smiling at me. I laughed. He was doing very well with the language. Better than my dad, who couldn't bear not being able to express himself as well in French as he did in English, couldn't 'lose face'. It's a big hurdle to get over.

When we eventually had a departure date for him, he busied himself packing his bags and the van, planning his route, booking his ticket and "generally futsing about", as he'd put it. After he left – we made it quick and clean to avoid the tears, at least in front of each other – I kept finding Post-it notes everywhere, with short, loving messages on – in the car, my filing cabinet, my handbag, amongst my soya and evening primrose capsules, under the computer cover ... He rang me from Clare's flat:

"Hello, darling. Things are going really well here. Clare's tiling.

---

[*] Another of his talents – he makes delicious *pâtisserie*. The local men are uneasy about this, though they praise his cakes. *"Mauvais exemple,"* they say, shaking their heads at him.

Phil's (current boyfriend) bricking up holes. I'm on soil pipes ..."

"Oh no, not bogs again, love (see Chapter 5). I thought we'd finished with those! Poor you. I'm sorry I'm not there helping. Bet it's not as hot as here though."

"No, it's raining. It does feel weird without you."

"I don't feel like I'm without you. I've found five notes so far. I'm thinking of you a lot. You 're so lovely, so thoughtful ..."

"I think there are a few more around," he said. I could hear the pleasure in his voice. "And there's a little something in a *Vignerons Ardechois* bag hanging up in the cellar."

"Oh, Mike, you're far too good for me, you know, my darling. I didn't get you anything. All I did was whinge about you going, told everyone you were **abandoning** me." (I had been jokingly melodramatic – what's that quote about truth in jest?)

"Oh, you weren't that bad. You just let me get on with it, which was the best thing. I do understand."

How typical of the man! Mike had treated my negative rants with his usual patience. He always outdoes me in the goodness department (mind you, it's not hard! Am I trying to exorcise some demons here? I must be listening to too much Joni Mitchell in his absence!) He hardly ever analyses or broods and is probably the better for it! A part of me had resented him having to make the trip – with all the upheaval, travel, time and expense involved. I doubt I would have done it. But then, I've never had kids, so I don't know about this unconditional love thing. But I do know how much support I got from my mum and dad. I also know how he feels about, and treats, his daughters, because I get so much of the same treatment. I am a big kid anyway and I've often teased him about taking me on as another daughter!

I also tease him about his parenting/rearing methods – kindness, discipline and time (plus lots of fun and love) is The Way-According-To-Mike. In the fifties, he won a second prize at Crufts with his dog, Brandy, a bull mastiff, and everyone cites Clare and Louise as near-perfect daughters (particularly compared with their contemporaries). He's the first to say that he certainly didn't raise them single-handed and that his wife Gill had as much to do with the way their offspring turned out as he had. But, whenever

WHITE KNIGHT IN A WHITE VAN

I hear parents complaining about their kids, I tell them to have a word with Mike, who has the knack – same treatment for dogs and kids – seems to work! The "something in the bag in the cellar", by the way, was a lead crystal heart, with the message: "This is like the real one I've left with you at La Clède where it belongs."

You must be sticking your fingers down your throats by now, but, heh, what do you think? Hardly a *mauvais exemple. Super exemple*, more like! He also said he'd be back before my birthday, in time to make me a cake! Two days before he was due, I was watering at the back of the house. It was early evening, cooler now after another hot day, and the garden was thirsty as usual. Suddenly the water stopped.

"Hello," I thought to myself, "what's happened now?" I turned round to look, and there he was behind me, grinning from ear to ear.

Again, my delighted shriek of "Mike, you're here!" *Déjà vu*, or what? It was like a rerun of the last time he'd surprised me for my birthday. We stood there and hugged one another for a long time. He looked tired, but very good (as usual) and obviously pleased to be 'home'. Just as before, the van was loaded with prezzies and other surprise goodies. The rest of the evening passed as if we were in a dream, and we kept touching each other – though we do that a lot anyway – to make sure it was all real. It was so great to be together again.

Back to the summer of 1997 and our temporary 'love nest' in Canterbury - and it **was** temporary - for one night only. We were told to leave the next morning by our friend, John's property manager, whom John had forgotten to inform of our stay. I think he thought we'd wandered in off the street! So, having nowhere else to go, we moved into Mike's cottage with its one cold tap and lav in the garden shed, and started stripping out. We bought a futon from our favourite Merchant Chandler shop (The Most Interesting Shop in Canterbury, says a sign on its exterior). What more did we need? Thank goodness it was August and warm!

After a fortnight, we'd got down to bare, damp walls – God knows how many layers of wallpaper we removed. We'd ripped out all the carpets and discovered the original and now highly dangerous lead wiring, badly sealed-off gas pipes and other such nasties, like dry rot under the floorboards. We were amazed the woman had survived so long in that time-bomb of a house. It certainly was an eye-opening example of the conditions in which some old people still live in the nineties in the affluent south-east of England, paying over-the-top council tax too, probably.

Only Mike would have considered it a bargain at £30,000 (which is all he had left to spend after the separation); only Mike would have taken it on. It was tiny – only 11ft wide! – a real two-up, two-down property, with a small garden backing onto the city wall and a lovely view of the cathedral from the rear upstairs room, in which we were sleeping but which would become the bathroom. But, for now, we'd finished. Mike arranged for a contact of his to come and redo the roof, and we were off south to the Ardèche again, to relieve our friends of house-sitting duties and see in more guests through into the autumn. That made three visits to Ribes for Mike that year.

He was now introduced as *mon mec* to all the curious friends and neighbours. As he spoke barely any French at first, it was up to me to let everyone know what a treasure I'd found. (They'd come to realise it themselves in time.) But for now, they just asked if we were happy to be in Ribes together again, and commented that I'd certainly waited long enough to find someone permanent.

"Vingt-cinq ans à peu près, mais ça valait l'attente!" (About twenty-five years but worth the wait!)

We were observed with interest, as we gardened, cleaned and DIYd together, pretty much unheard of here in the country, as the women do women's jobs and the men do men's. And we **were** nearly always together. We must have looked happy. Everyone seemed to smile at us – the check-out ladies at Champion supermarket, normally very sullen-faced, the stallholders in the market: *"Ah, voici les amoureux,"* they'd exclaim, as we walked by or stopped to buy our bread, olives, *saucissons* and fruit and veg. The town was much quieter now, as most of the visitors and tourists had left, so we were more noticeable. But something charmed was going on; I'd never felt so much a part of everything and it was such fun to share it. Mike was so motivated, drinking it all in, trying everything and wanting to be a part of it all too.

"Thank you for giving me all this, Jan – a whole new life. I think it's wonderful how they all greet us. I want them to get to know me, to know I'm with you and that I live here with you. I Only Want To Be With You.*" (Mike's a big Dusty Springfield fan – now, there's a bit of a song title clue!)

The autumn days, once the last guests had gone and again we had the place to ourselves, were just a delight. The garden could take a breather after the long, hot summer, though there was plenty of pruning to keep me happy and bonfires to keep Mike happy. The sun kept on shining, of course, and on days when the *mistral* wind blows fresh and cool from the Alps, the light is so clear and bright on the trees and vines, now changing to yellows, reds and oranges, you stand and stare in awe at the beauty of it all and count your blessings. This is the light that brought all those painters.

Mike loved his first experience of the *vendange*, the grape harvest, and watched with pleasure as friends and families all worked together in the vineyards, filling up the small, wooden carriers with bunches of plump, black grapes and carrying them in twos to tip them into the tractor trailers. The locals really enjoy this time of year too – it's an important event in their year. I've never seen more contented faces than those of the farmers, driving their tractors of grapes to the *Caves Cooperatives*, to add theirs to the huge vats of Gamay, Merlot, Syrrah and Cabernet – the reward for all the hard work.

We did a lot of walking, sometimes up in the chestnut and pine woods, sometimes by the river. I wanted to show Mike more of the local sights and discover new ones together. We'd always find things to bring back, huge pine cones, unusual bits of wood, small rocks that grabbed our attention. They're so varied round here – it's a geologist's dream. I'd always forget to take bags; Mike wouldn't. Like all the locals, we went mushrooming, chestnut

---

*One of his Christmas presents from me that year was a T-shirt with 07 on the back and *J'habite ici* (I live here) on the front!

picking – two kids in paradise, enjoying the fruits of the land.

Then it rained, and it rained and rained – solidly for three whole days. The sound of rushing water was everywhere, as it poured down steps and paths, into the roads and the water channels. But it was the river valley that took our breath away, transformed into a magical Waterworld. The rock faces gushed; there were cascades and waterfalls all around. The river was so swollen, up by at least two metres, so that beaches and shrubs entirely disappeared. It had changed colour from a slow-flowing blue/green to a seething torrent of brown and white foam, as it swept around the bends.

"This is when the real canoeists come out," I said. "Do you fancy having a go?"

"Yes, but not when it's quite as rough as this perhaps. But we'll do it, eh? We'll just carry on doing lots of things we like, won't we?" We hugged each other; we like to do that too!

There's always a down side. Not only did the roof leak in our side of the house, in the usual place down the party wall, but in quite a number of places in the *gîte* side too, but only at the rear, it seemed; the front half was still OK. This roof hadn't been touched by my parents, as the surveyor had said it was sound when they bought the house. But that was over thirty years ago at least, with no record of when it last had any attention, beyond a bit of tile shifting and replacement. It was time to get the buckets and the newspapers out, close up the houses, pray and head north. We had a house to do up in Canterbury.

We worked on Mike's 'ruin' all through the winter and by early spring it was finished and let. It really did look good – letting it was not a problem (just the tenant, as it turned out, but it's too ugly a tale to tell here). We'd added a conservatory behind and put the garden back into some sort of shape – the agent described it as a "delightful bijou cottage". Our first guests of 1998 were due in Ribes in mid-June. Before that, Mike had convinced me that together we could reroof the rear of the *gîte*!

And I believed him!

- 4 -
STILL CRAZY AFTER FIFTY YEARS (1998)

IT WAS TO BE the first year we would both stay in France for the whole summer. We drove down in early May with two vehicles, each full to the brim. Mike had two bikes, six long square posts and four packs of shingle tiles on top of his Bedford van, parts for a covered pergola to be built over the rear terrace of the *gîte*. (We hadn't been able to find these items in the French builders' merchants.) I had a flat-pack garden seat and wheelbarrow – great bargains, courtesy of B&Q – on top of my Renault 5! We struggled in second gear up all the hills!

Now work was to start big-time on both houses – a gradual, but complete overhaul of the *gîte* – we simply couldn't get away just with decorating any longer* – and major works on the other side to make it into 'our' home. After all, it was the only bit of property either of us owned that we didn't let out! Looking back five years later at what we've accomplished under Mike's leadership – I'm only mentioning the major things in this book, and we've done everything ourselves – I find it totally unbelievable, but yet more evidence of his drive and super-productivity.

We broke our journey at Montargis, south of Paris. I knew a hotel in the centre that had a locked courtyard for safe parking, where I'd stayed before on my visits to Ribes with Alan and friends, Ron and Gerry. It's one of those typical French hotels (pre-Formule 1 and the rest), which have dodgy plumbing and gaudy, patterned wallpaper on every wall and ceiling, which hasn't been matched quite right, endless stairs and dark corridors with *minuterie* lights, and communal loos and showers. The whole place

---

* Or my well-used ploy of saying, "I'm so grateful the distressed look's in," as I plied guests with another *kir*! (White wine and fruit liqueur.)

smells of cooking and coffee and *Gauloises* cigarettes. They should make them listed. They're dying out.

The nearby old part of Montargis is full of waterways – a little Venice of canals and river and a cool and peaceful place to walk through after a day's driving. We strolled around, arm in arm, making plans and discussing the projects planned for the summer. We spotted an old lantern in an *Antiquités* shop window.

"That'd look great at La Clède, wouldn't it", Mike said. "Let's come back tomorrow before we leave and see what they want for it." We bought it – 50FF – a snip, and then left Montargis on the familiar old N7 south.

Once I leave the N102 at the Col de la Chavade and head off over the plateau to descend to Ribes, through the Tanargue mountain range and the beautiful, rocky Beaume valley, I get high as a kite. Mike too now. We're tired from driving, we're only just over an hour from Ribes, the scenery is stunning, the mountainsides covered in bright yellow gorse – and the brakes start overheating because we're so loaded! Take it gently, we'll soon be there. But you absolutely can't look around; you've got to watch the road, which is treacherously winding with sheer drops, so if you meet a lorry (quite likely), you've got to be concentrating.

We finally arrive and drive up the ramp into the welcoming courtyard, which is full of colour, lilac and roses in bloom, other plants and trees bursting with life; the gravel's full of weeds. It's always the same for me – I rush up the steps to the garden straight away, doing a mental inventory, seeing what's survived the winter. Next it's the houses. The first checkover reveals no awful disasters *in absentia*. It has rained quite a lot, the stained newspaper covers reveal, but it's nevertheless now dry inside both houses. Elation! It seems we've survived another winter; all seems well. (It's only when you go round the second time that the elation turns to despair, as you realise all that needs to be done!)

And we certainly had a lot on our plate. We had just over five weeks before our first guests, in which to:

- reroof half the *gîte* – Fixing A Hole (or six at least, where the rain gets in)

- rebuild and cover the chimney and improve the roof fillets with the party wall

- construct a covered pergola over the *gîte*'s rear terrace, treat and stain it
- build a stone BBQ to fit the kit we'd brought with us, enlarge the terrace area, and, if time
- give the kitchen a bit of a makeover.

Plus, spring-clean the place and get the garden looking more managed – grass cut, paths and steps weeded, pots potted up with geraniums and petunias, garden furniture cleaned and varnished, hammocks up! And the rest – the list seemed very long indeed! We started with the worst, the roof.

We'd discovered a brilliant new product called *Flexotuille* the year before. If only it had been around in 1995 when "The Roofers of Ribes" did 'our' roof, we'd be totally confident it wouldn't leak again in our lifetime. But, because ours was redone the old-fashioned way with just pantiles resting on rafters, it's already showing the strain, and so probably will!

Flexotuilles are large, 4x8ft sheets of waterproofed material (tarred on the underside), corrugated to accommodate pantiles. They're tough, light and bendy and just perfect for the irregular roof timbers in these old houses. The main beams, joists and rafters in the *gîte* are round – originally tree trunks and branches. They were all still sound, it appeared, but we treated them anyway, as we worked across the roof. The sheets are pinned, overlapping, to the rafters, and cemented over on the ridge and at the edges. And Bob's your Builder! You end up with a completely waterproof roof before a tile is laid. The tiles protect and decorate only.

So, Mike, his vertigo suppressed once again, was pretty much permanently up on the roof. My main job was to feed him with anything he required, that is, *Flexotuilles*, batts of insulation and tools (light); buckets of cement and hods of tiles (heavy), while, simultaneously, seeing to the removal of the considerable debris. All this via a system of ladders and a borrowed *tour* (scaffold tower), set up behind the house. So I was up and down like a yo-yo, undoubtedly moaning a lot of the time! It actually all went remarkably smoothly, but very sweatily, as it was extremely hot most days.

Now, heaving cement and tiles up two storeys is no mean feat for a 'gal' – I just can't understand why I've developed cellulite on my arms! But it's like most building projects, I've found – the thought of doing is far, far worse than actually doing, especially when you're working with someone who knows what he's about, though, as Mike would say, he's no professional roofer. I just had/have infinite confidence in him – he has heaps of patience, common sense and experience of making. It works every time. And so did we, and how.

Two other indispensable building products, as far as I can see, as apprentice *manoeuvre* (builder's mate), are Gripfill, which fills and sticks anything to anything, and which we affectionately call gunk, and Unibond, a PVA adhesive, which you add to cement mixtures, to improve adhesion and waterproofing. This magic solution, in both senses of the word, was slapped all over the concrete fillets with the party wall and the sides of the rebuilt chimney, which had been leaking badly into the fireplace below; gunk was applied wherever anything needed to stay put! As with the final touch to the large, square chimney. What to cover it with to keep out the rain?

One of the answers to this vital question, in these parts, apart from pitched pantiles or unattractive, made-for-this-purpose *briques,* is to use a piece of *schiste* rock (shale), called *lauzes* when used as roofing slates. Some of the old houses in the Ardèche and the neighbouring Lozère are still roofed like this, but like everywhere, these old building skills are disappearing, and manufactured tiles are replacing them. The Ribes part of our mountain is *grès* (sandstone); St André, the next village a few kilometers higher up, happens to sit on *schiste.* Any geologist would explain why far better than I, but it's obviously something to do with huge pressures and rock movements hundreds of thousands of years ago.

Both covered head-to-toe in grey cement – Mike with additional red dust from cutting terracotta tiles with his angle-grinder – and armed with a bolster and club hammer (heavy-duty rock breaking tools), we jumped into the Renault and went slate hunting around St André. We couldn't have been more conspicuous for people not wanting to be seen pillaging the countryside! We thought it would be a relatively simple job to find a piece that had already dropped from the rock face, or was lying in a pile from fallen walls[*]. We searched for ages, driving up and down, but none of the stones was large enough to cover our chimney hole. Finally, in desperation, Mike attacked the rock face itself. Applying brute force in the right place is very often the perfect solution to a problem, in his experience. And as *schiste* is formed in layers like slate, it wasn't actually that hard to split a piece off. But it was too big to go into the boot of the car! We had to chip bits off until it would fit. We could barely lift it together – it probably weighed about fifty kilos – and it had to be cut down still further before it could be raised – no mean feat, I might add – to sit on the chimneytop and be gunked in place.

Another of the old roofing traditions locally is to decorate both the ends of the roof and the tops of chimneys with an upright-standing, phallic – and thus probably, pagan – stone. These mini menhirs also have to be searched for – obviously the bigger and more phallic the better! However, we found a rather modest, triangular one for the chimney, not wanting to offend the neighbours, and what did we stick it on with? Gunk, of course!

Well pleased with the results of our labours and relieved that the hardest and most important job was over, we tackled the next items on the action list. The covered pergola was built, using the posts and shingle tiles we'd brought and *coffrage*[**] (cheap shuttering boards from the local builders' merchants), sanded and

---

[*] These terrace walls, all hand-built, cover the mountainsides like giant steps, and border nearly all the roads round here – there are kilometres and kilometres of them. Their purpose, obviously, was/is to retain the land and permit cultivation of trees and other crops, after the land was handed out, post-Revolution – some probably even long before that – so they're centuries old. With people migrating to towns and land falling into disuse, many are unfortunately falling down, though some are being rebuilt.

[**] We've used this to make so many things, including much of our furniture. Planed, sanded and stained with dark brown *brou de noix* (walnut juice), our cupboards and bookshelves look like antiques!

stained bottle green. It worked well, although we were aware that it was out of character. The usual local method for building a covered, external living/dining area (an *auvent*) was a more substantial affair with heavy timber or stone pillars and a timber and tile roof. The *gîte*'s rear terrace was not large enough to warrant such a construction, and all we wanted was a shady dining area and somewhere for people to sit outside if it was raining.

The summer thunderstorms are often a spectacular entertainment, especially at night, with streaks of lightning repeatedly filling the black, rumbling sky, emptying its contents over the valleys and forest-covered mountains visible from the house. In summer, you can hear the hot land hiss* as it laps it up. As it seems to rain less and less these days, I am always mightily relieved to see it and spend ages watching from **our** covered terrace (built three years later), dancing to the rain god and saying, "Thankyou, thankyou! Shan't have to water for a bit!" With this pergola, we had a height restriction and guttering to contend with, so its roof, instead of being pitched, had to be curved, which gave it a sort of pagoda look. People walking past on the road above noticed and commented favourably to us on how unusual it was. We don't know what they really thought of it but, five years or so down the line, they are at least used to it!

The stone BBQ was built against one of the garden walls. The terrace was enlarged, which meant the existing retaining wall had to be built up, and then the area gravelled. A second dining table and chairs were added under the large *boule acacia* tree that Peg had had planted there. It's a pleasant, cool spot at any time of day but it does have one drawback. It's on the upper floor of the *gîte*, so all the paraphernalia for eating has to be *schlepped* on trays up the stairs and down again. We've thought about pulleys and 'dumb waiters', but as yet have not been able to come up with a satisfactory solution. We can only hope our guests have enough energy to do this! But it is private, especially now that we've put up a split-bamboo screen along the boundary with our perhaps

---

* *The Hissing of Summer Lawns,* Joni's eighth album. The water comes from sprinklers though; it is America after all!

too curious and friendly neighbour to the side, who replaced Mr Mettayer – Albert from Alsace – the other owner of the party wall. At the front of the house, we also had to devise some method of splitting up the long terrace common to both houses, to give guests – and ourselves – more privacy. Easy peasy for Mr Fix-It. He just knocked up a couple of wooden troughs with trellises incorporated, over which we trained the virginia creeper that covered our terrace. (And while he was at it, he enlarged and reroofed the *marquise* (open porch) over the old oak front door!) With this new arrangement, we were close to guests if they wanted to socialise, or ask for information, but we could also keep a much lower profile it they didn't! The external work to the house was done for now. Time for us to move indoors and give the kitchen its much-needed facelift.

In *Lilac and Roses*, Peg describes the frustrations she had with the kitchen decor. There are some attractive blue and white tiles around the old-fashioned cooking area next to the fireplace. It's an interesting and attractive original feature. Hot embers would be removed from the fire and placed in the three small metal braziers set in the tiles, on which pans were placed for heating or keeping food warm. (The ashes dropped into a recess beneath.) She'd always wanted, being particularly fond of blue and white china, to follow this through in the colour scheme. When looking for reasonably inexpensive kitchen furniture in the area in the late sixties, however, she'd found the choice somewhat limited.

Of course, it was nothing remotely like what's happened since, with Habitat, Ikea and the like offering so many lovely things in natural materials. Formica was very big then! French housewives were keen to alter dark, old kitchen areas, whose design hadn't changed much in centuries, with modern colours and materials. In the 'department stores' of Alès and Aubenas, there were two colourways for the units – white/grey marble effect and bottle green. She very reluctantly plumped for a three-door, three-drawer bottle green one and changed her scheme to green and yellow instead.

I was keen to create her original choice. We covered the dark green tiles above the sink and worktops with new Delft-type, blue and white ones. Existing yellow wallcupboard doors were painted blue, as was the fifties 'pull-down', and wooden knobs replaced the chrome handles. Courtesy of Mike, we had two extra cupboards of his in stripped pine to add to the furniture, and he made a 'Welsh dresser' top for one of them. But what on earth could we do with the green Formica? Mike came up with one more brilliant idea. The pine furniture looked so good and had provided the inspiration the previous year at the end of the season to clad the Formica with *lambris* (tongue and groove pine strips) and tile the worktop in white. We had then asked his mate, Derek the carpenter back in England to make us some new doors and drawer fronts. (This is Derek's speciality, making furniture from salvaged pine floorboards.) We covered the chimneybreast with a collection of assorted blue and white china. The whole scheme really did work a treat, and I only wish Peg could have seen it.

It was time for a bit of R and R (rest and recuperation). We were expecting Clare, Mike's younger daughter – her first visit, for a week, with a friend. It's always a pleasure to share something you love with someone you love, and we made full use of our free-er time, bathing in our lovely river Beaume and in friends' swimming pools – as the temperatures soared at the end of June[*]. We always get lots of invites to use pools, but actually prefer the river, where we can skinnydip and dry off naked in the warm, early morning sunshine. After a few delicious hours of sunning, reading and flopping again and again into the water to cool off, you head for the shade of an acacia tree with the picnic lunch.

It's a typical rocky mountain river, that tumbles over short rapids, into small pools like natural *jacuzzis*, then slows down in deeper, wider channels, that are perfect for swimming. Occasional sandy beaches slope down into the soft, clean water, full of trout and carp which nibble your toes as you stand at the water's edge poised to rush or dive in. Mike prefers a longer, more sedate entry, but Clare and Tracey were rushers like me! The wooded

---

[*] For the last two years, actually, June has been as hot as August. Is it global warming, the earth turning on its axis? Whatever, it's something else for me to worry about!

mountains rise up sheer each side, and apart from the odd, ancient house, perched on an outcrop, there is no other sign of civilisation. Buzzards, hawks and herons fly high overhead and if you're lucky you'll see the kingfisher, the beaver and a red squirrel or two.

5 July 1998 – my fiftieth birthday. (I was born in Bradford, Yorkshire just after midnight on the first day of the National Health Service, so my mum didn't have to pay the doctor!)

Comme célébration, Mike and I are throwing a small garden party – very English! We have an equal mix of English and French guests, totalling fourteen in all. (My lucky number is seven.) French: Balazuc neighbours, Christian and Roberte, daughters Vladia and Orane, (all three women are stunning); Marcelle Nicholas, my south-west neighbour (after twenty odd years, she still hasn't said we could *se tutoyer* – old style formal – wears floral pinny frocks you see in the markets, but lovely with it), and Jeff (actually Jean-François, J-F) and Renée, some more worldly friends from the next mountain along! English: Mike and I, Roger and Pat (not bad looking, either!) Bellis*, and another couple, some friends who were staying with them at the time, and Margaret, a friend of my parents and mine, who lives in nearby Paysac and who, with her husband Michael, were a fantastic help and support to me when I started letting La Clède to holiday-makers.

It was fun decorating the garden. We put red, white and blue flags and streamers between the trees – very handy that both countries have the same coloured flags – with co-ordinating balloons and "Happy 50th" banners, and occasional seats and tables around the 'lawn'. (A large sign which read *Attention aux fourmis!* – Beware of the ants! – identified the only out of bounds area, a huge nest.) We had a large trestle table in the shade, covered with red, white and blue crêpe paper and the food spread, and bottles of champagne in a dustbin full of ice. The food consisted of traditional Ardèche *apéro* fare – the usual nibbles, *chips* and nuts, pizza

---

* I met them in Champion supermarket, Joyeuse one morning and we've been friends since.

and quiche, *saucissons*, olives, cheeses – plus one English educational item, cucumber sandwiches (with crusts), and large bowls of peaches, nectarines and apricots. Mike made a super-duper chocolate birthday cake; rather, two chocolate cakes, one with a 5, the other with 0 in icing sugar, sifted through a template on top. The 'do' was due to kick off at 18.30 hours.

They were still there at nine o'clock, which I took to be a good sign, though I could feel a hunting argument coming on between Christian and Renée, who's a fanatical nature lover and green to the core. As I've said, Christian lives to hunt, and it is a tradition in rural France that goes way back. As we all probably know, things are slow to change in the country, no matter what country, and 'outsiders' (that is, not *gens du pays*) and their well-meaning(?) opinions tend not to be very well received by the long-standing locals. Town Man vs Country Man.

The arguments are not that different from those going on at the moment in England, except generally here they eat everything they kill. Hunting in rural France is still a way of life for so many people with a link with the land, which is much more everybody's, post-Revolution, than is the case in Britain. There, it is viewed as more of a sport for toffs, even though the farmers are a large part of it, and it's more egalitarian than that. There's still the hierarchy, of course – the Establishment at the top.

There's an enormous hunting debate going on in France too. In the Ardèche, the *sangliers* (wild boar) are now so numerous, they are becoming a nuisance and causing an awful lot of damage to properties, particularly to the land-retaining terrace walls that cover every mountainside and on which crop production depends. The hunters have been feeding them, leaving corn and then returning to take pops at them. More serious than that, though, is that some hunters are breeding and cross-breeding them – both illegal – with the domestic pig, so that now instead of the sows having only one or two *marcassins* ('boarlets'?), they're having broods of six and upwards. And even more serious is that contents of freezers, ie a huge surplus of butchered boar meat, is now being dumped in the countryside, as are the unwanted parts of freshly shot boar. This certainly helps keep the fly count up!

Hunters are not noted for leaving places as they find them. Graffiti is starting to appear against these *cochongliers (cochons/sangliers)* and the men who prey on them.

The packs of hunting dogs, of which more in Chapter 10, are only ever let out of their pens when their owners hunt. Consequently, on these occasions, once the dogs are out of the vehicles and in the woods, they think all their Christmases have come at once and rush madly off, ignoring all whistles, horns and calls to attention. The fact of the matter is that, apart from the really serious hunters who know what they're doing like Christian, their owners spend most of the day looking for their dogs and not actually doing much hunting at all! (There are also quite a lot of accidents as they shoot anything that moves.) It's much more about the men being with their mates, looking macho with their guns, and after the day's 'hunting', hanging out at the *cabanons* (hunting lodges is really too grand a word – 'hunting shacks'), to which they return with or without prey to drink and bond some more. If they have shot a boar or two – there are actually so many it's hard to miss! – they carve the prey up and share it out, and maybe finish the day with a barbecue, (though it takes about an hour to collect wood and make the fire, and only a couple of minutes to 'cook' the flesh. They like it *bleu*, or nearly raw – barely one minute each side!) Nevertheless, they take it all very, very seriously and being *Président de la Société de Chasse* is a real honour and **the** status symbol for the men.

Just before *la rentrée*, the start of the autumn school term, we'd arranged with Bernadette, a friend from nearby Les Vans to help her move some of her belongings to Nice, where she'd landed a new teaching post at one of the *lycées*, and had purchased an apartment. Once again, the faithful Bedford van was loaded to bursting point, beds and mattresses on the roof, and off we set. It's further than it looks on the map and we couldn't travel that quickly, so we arrived at the *rendez-vous* late afternoon, some two hours after Bernadette in her car. Inclined to paranoia anyway and convinced something terrible had happened to us and to all her stuff, she was extremely pleased to see us when we finally turned up at her aunt's beautiful house just outside Biot.

We left the van there and walked with overnight bags to the charming hotel she'd booked for us in the central square of the village. It's a very pleasant place – all the houses decorated with colourful hanging baskets and windowboxes – though it's a tad too gentrified and touristy for our taste. It has attracted many artists and artisans, especially potters and glass blowers, so their wares are on sale everywhere. The difference in affluence, compared with the Ardèche, was particularly striking and the house prices astronomical. Water shortages are extremely common in high summer and the status-symbol lawns are likely replaced every year, we were told! We'd been invited to return in the evening to have a meal with the family, which included Bernadette's cousin, Guy, chief of police for Nice, and his wife. It's common in these parts to have a complete, second kitchen outside, as so many meals are taken out of doors. Guy was in charge of the steaks – like the hunters, a quick thirty seconds either side – tac/tac, he called it. There was much amusement about this. The English are said by the French to murder their meat twice, the second time in the pan! The following day, Guy was to prove an extremely useful contact when helping Bernadette with her move.

He said he would escort us and the van with its precious cargo to her new apartment in the centre of Nice. We could barely keep up with him. Siren blaring and travelling at speeds of up to 80kph through the 50kph zones and the odd red light, we arrived breathless at the classy new *Résidence*. Parking looked like it would be a problem, but not to Guy, who put his car on a zebra crossing and then, having instructed someone else to vacate a space, signalled to us to take it! Oh, the power and the glory of it all, if only fleeting!

We were moving on to Menton after installing Bernadette, to stay with an old friend of mine, Daevid, ex-DJ and now French sports correspondent for the Beeb. Mike hadn't visited the Côte d'Azur before, so we took the scenic coast road, famous from so many movies. Since the opening of the more impersonal but definitely quicker *autoroute,* this is quiet enough to allow a leisurely drive and the opportunity to enjoy the spectacular scenery. But I was appalled at the amount of new housing everywhere; most of the towns had definitely gone downmarket. Nice seafront we found particularly unappetising, looking more like Margate with its one-armed bandit emporia, fast food outlets and litter. How the mighty have fallen. Monaco didn't tempt us, but Menton, first time for both of us, seemed a lot more genteel, retaining more of its English influences than Nice. Not that we're happier amid Englishness, but it was a lot less commercialised – and cleaner. With beautiful beaches and tropical gardens, an impressive Old Town of golden buildings and Belle Epoque villas, it has a perfect climate, mild even in February, when it celebrates its Lemon Festival.

Daevid and his partner Carol had once stayed at La Clède – 'Jan's side' – when it only had one-star! We had a lot more comfort *chez eux* than they'd experienced here. They were great hosts, Daevid insisting that only he was allowed in the kitchen and also treating us to a day out in Italy, to the huge market at Vintimille and to an enormous, belt-loosening lunch in a *trattoria* near Vallebona. Where do they put all that food, these Continentals?! Among the things that struck us on this trip was the complete absence of a frontier – the customs building was deserted. (When will Britain get around to thinking of itself, if only in a small way, as part of Europe? That Channel is one helluva barrier.) Secondly, a significant drop in the level of affluence, the upkeep of build-ings, the shops and so on in this part of Italy, in contrast to the opulence along the south coast of France. There seemed to be women riding Vespa scooters everywhere – in France they can afford cars. I kept on thinking of Eddie Izzard and his sketch on what it means to be European,[*] where he mimes riding a scooter, repeatedly saying, *"Ciao"*!

We had a slow but magnificent drive back north up through the Var. Leaving Menton, after a quick flip westbound on the *autoroute* with its impressive tunnels and viaducts, we turned north and followed the Var river valley, the road crossing and recrossing the river and the railway, up into Provence. How arid it was there; all traces of water seemed to have vanished and the

---

[*] Eddie Izzard talking to an American audience about The European Dream on *Dress To Kill* video (Virgin, 1998)

countryside was brown and burnt. Even the famous lavender fields looked sad. We were extremely glad to get back home to the green and peasant, no pleasant (Freudian slip!) Ardèche and to an imminent visit from my brother Ian and his wife Tina, who'd decided to use some of their air miles and fly to Montpellier.

We went down to fetch them from the airport late afternoon, having checked out and reserved a table at a *Les Routiers* restaurant, *Le Mistral*, on the way. These eateries, principally for truck drivers, usually serve excellent food, particularly at midday, the main French eating time. This was evening, though, and the restaurant was deserted; we were the only diners, save one other solitary man. Next door in the bar, however, there was a country & western *soirée* going on and the place was packed with wannabe cowboys, all trying to socialise over the din of the music, which blasted out every time the door opened, as the waitress brought our boiled-in-the-bag food. It was all a bit surreal and we felt rather out of place! To top the evening, we had the mother of all storms as we drove back to Ribes. It was such a downpour, we could hardly see the road. But at least we knew that the *gîte* no longer leaked!

Another cat entered our lives. Min had been adopted (and spayed) by one of our neighbours, Rosy, who lives in Marseille and owns a holiday home in our hamlet, where she stays with her family for a few months each summer. So Min now led a double life and grew fatter on regular food and domesticity, rather than pregnancy. Meanwhile, Roberte Balazuc, never one to turn away a hungry mouth, had been feeding a beautiful blonde stray, which like most female ferals was serially pregnant. It was Christian's job to dispose of the litters. This is the way here – spaying a cat is regarded as a waste of money, unless it's a real family pet. In the most recent litter, one kitten had been missed and duly appeared soon after with its mother. There were arguments in the Balazuc household, three women for keeping the kitten, one man against. But, he couldn't resist his daughters' wishes. Besides, the kitten was adorable, white with grey and pink/beige patterns, and everyone, including us, was enchanted when they saw her.

"Qu'est-ce qu'elle est mignonne (cute)," we all said, looking curi-

ously at Christian to discover why she was still alive. We knew how adamant he was about stray cats, being a dog man, too.

"*Je l'ai pas vue, celle-ci,*" he said. (I missed this one.)

"*Mais, on va la garder,*" said Vladia, smiling triumphantly at her father. (We're going to keep her.)

We were told the story of her salvation.

"*Mais, elle a de la chance,*" I said. "*Vous devez l'appeler Lucky.*"

"*Oui, on a pensé à ça!*" Orane cried. "*Lucky sera bien son nom, hein?*" (We thought of that. We'll call her Lucky.) They all agreed.

The Balazuc household was often empty – Christian at the bank, Roberte and Vladia both nurses (Vladia still training) and Orane at college. So Lucky came to spend a lot of time with us as she grew bolder. Alone – her mother couldn't make friends; she was too wild and moved on, never to be seen again. Lucky loved the garden, like Min had. It's full of hidey-holes in which to sleep and hunt, and we were always there with a caress and a tit-bit. We became official surrogate parents. The first time she curled up and slept on a human lap – Mike's – was a big step towards domesticity. She was a stylist's dream, looking absolutely adorable wherever she chose to put herself, her colouring perfectly complementing the shades of stone in the house and garden. And our guests loved her too. I took loads of photos of her and at Christmas sent the other 'parents' a 1999 calendar with a different pose for each month. They still have it hanging in their kitchen in 2003!

When all the guests had gone for the year, we had a visit from Mike's two sisters, Betty and Dru. They'd both been to France before; indeed, Betty's husband Maurice Dumas had French nobility connections! But they hadn't been so far south and were amazed how warm and pleasant the climate was in late September, early October, though the temperature plummets with the disappearance of the sun. We took them on some sightseeing tours to the famous Ardèche Gorges and to some of the fascinating medieval villages around here, but for the most part, they were happy to enjoy the garden, taking full advantage of the painters' light to do some watercolours.

After their departure, the sunny October days continued until one extremely heavy rainstorm took us by surprise. So heavy that it brought down part of one of the terrace walls in the garden. This had already happened to some of the same wall before my parents' time, but they'd never really had the energy to repair it themselves or the money to spend on what they thought was not a real necessity. There were steps up beside the house anyway to get from one level to another. My brother and friend Alan had once had a half-hearted attempt at rebuilding it during a stay at Ribes, on one of their European tours as students, but it had remained a pile of stones and earth – a bit of an eyesore to be honest – and any attempts to turn it into a rockery never succeeded very well.

Mike decided to take on this huge landscaping challenge – he likes a challenge! He started drystone wall building – a first for him – with a vengeance, repairing the latest *chute* (fall) in a day, and then began to build a ramp, joining the two remaining upright bits of wall, in place of the pile of stones and earth. I was appalled at the size of the task. He promised only to work on it in small doses, two to three hours max at a time. He finally finished cobbling it in 2001. He's created many *œuvres d'art* in his life. This one is his legacy at La Clède.

- 5 -
DO YOU TIP THE DUNNY MAN? (1999)

IF YOU THOUGHT last year was a busy DIY one, there's more to come, I'm afraid! This year, we arrived in the Ardèche just after Easter to find snow on the plateau. It looked very beautiful, as snow always does, but it's not so good if you're driving up and down 1:8 mountain roads! So we gave our usual route down the Beaume valley a miss, in preference to the more major, busier road down the Ardèche valley. Both descents are breathtaking in more senses than one. I'd never been to Ribes so early before, so this white winter landscape was a new experience. The lower we got, the more the snow had melted and only the drifts on the northern mountain slopes remained. In the valley the sun was shining, the sky was blue; the lilacs, spring bulbs and flowers were blooming. Places and people were coming alive again after the winter 'hibernation'.

Usual elation upon arrival at La Clède, until we discovered that we'd had quite a few furry visitors – mice or dormice (*loirs*) that live in the walls and roofs – inside the house. I was used to seeing a few droppings around after the winter months, but most wildlife would leave once the house became occupied again. This was different. We looked around the kitchen where there was most damage – a few pieces of china and glasses broken and lots of droppings, and it wasn't hard to discover the cause. The previous year after some party or other we'd been given some leftovers in a round bread loaf, which had had its top cut off and centre removed, leaving just the crust in the form of a bowl. I'd left it in the hot sun and it had baked so hard it was almost like ceramic. This was now a small pile of crumbs and droppings on a shelf; it was what they'd been after when they were cold and hungry.

We cleared up superficially, too tired to do more, but the following day, while Mike went round the house, filling every possible hole with gunk (what else?!), I springcleaned the kitchen and contents. Once our side of the house was liveable in again – we have peasant standards! – we continued with the *gîte's* facelift, where the standards had to be somewhat higher. We decorated all walls white, upstairs and down, stained and varnished wooden ceilings, beams and floors and replaced some of the more dated fabrics and rugs. Both bathrooms were given an overhaul. But the floor of the downstairs lounge/diner was to prove a much harder transformation to effect. The problem was that two-thirds of it were the original terracotta tiles in the lounge area, and one-third was a cement floor at a slightly higher level. This was because of changes to the internal partition walls that my parents had had done to create a dining alcove.

My mum had spent a good few hours of her time down on her knees on the tiles with the Cardinal Red polish, but had finally abandoned this in favour of cord carpet throughout. We, of course, being suckers for punishment, wanted to re-expose the tiles, which it has to be said were in pretty bad shape. Many were cracked, but worse, they were covered, all around the edges of the room, in the plaster cement from the walls, which Geo and Serge had neglected to clear up. By the time Peg and Alan had arrived for the summer, this had set so hard it was unremovable. They had tried valiantly, but it proved too difficult a task for them and their limited tools and know-how. Mike thought sulphuric acid might do it!

"What, neat?" I asked, aghast.

"Well, OK, let's try it slightly diluted first."

We opened all the windows, donned masks and thick industrial rubber gloves and got on down. As usual, the thought of doing is worse than the doing, but it wasn't a nice job, and a combination of the solution and heavy-duty wire wool made no impression whatsoever on the cement. It stayed firmly stuck to the tiles. We went full-strength. Slight improvement, but in the end we too became fed up with it – chipping it off took far too long. Meanwhile, the tiles had never been so clean!

Our finish treatment to the cement floor was two coats of terracotta emulsion and two of floor varnish. A weaker solution of the paint was washed over the tiles, and the stubborn cement marks acquired some colour. The whole tiled floor was then covered in a sealer. It wasn't a bad result at all, considering what we were working with, and most of it was covered up afterwards with two large rugs, one an auction sale Axminster, a present from Mike's sister Betty, the other a beige cotton dhurry from India via Ikea. The old 'gold' cord carpet was recycled in the corridor and occasional bedroom upstairs.

A few other homey touches were added from Mike's stock of bits and pieces, most of which came from all the various houses he'd renovated over the years. He's always been an avid collector of all sorts of 'old stuff' from white glass light shades and porcelain light fittings to eye baths and saltcellars, and these all became part of the decor, together with other knick-knacks like plates and jugs (picked up cheap at *brocantes)*, crocheted mats (only 1FF from the *fripes* second-hand stall at the market. (If you've the patience to sort through the piles of garments and household fabrics and linens, you find some real bargains. The stuff comes to the Catholic Church from affluent countries like Switzerland, Germany and Austria and is sold at auction in bulk to the dealers. It's a very flourishing trade and can become quite addictive if you let it!) By the beginning of May, the *gîte* had never looked better and was ready for our first guests of the year.

Now it was time to start on some serious improvements to our side, bearing in mind that we couldn't do anything too noisy, building-wise, while our guests were in residence. We'd heard tales from some of them about previous stays on 'building sites' and we thought that just wasn't fair on people on holiday. Electrical wiring is a quiet job and Mike set to improving the extremely basic set-up *chez nous*, putting in a ring main and other modernisations (like an earth!) and hiding some of the cable runs. He said the wiring was a complete nightmare. For example, the mystery of two wires to a wall light fitting. Neither wire – tested first with a meter then with a wet finger (don't try this at home!) – was live. But, when connected to a bulb, it lit up. He's never worked it out! The various electricians who'd worked at the house over the years had created a major enigma. None of the wire colours matched up and it was next to impossible to follow a run. They just seemed to have used whatever colour wire was to hand!

When our guests went out on their trips, we made furniture outside in the courtyard. We needed more storage now there were two of us. So we cobbled up cupboards, using old doors we already had or acquired, and sanded and stained *coffrage*, as I described earlier. So busy, busy working to feather our nest! But we had a few days of play too, when we had a no-guests week. Ron and Gerry were on holiday with some friends of theirs at another Chez Nous *gîte* in Caux in Languedoc. We headed west in mid-June with a cake to celebrate Gerry's birthday a second time in France. We were also curious to check out some of the competition! Harold and Barbara with two small boys and another baby on the way had bought their town house with barn about six years before. The house hadn't needed much work, so Harold had been able to start almost immediately on the barn conversion to *gîtes*, which, like ours, would bring them in vital income.

The barn building beside the house, with a small courtyard linking the two, was exactly the same size as La Clède, about 12m x 4m and on three floors. Harold had turned the barn into three independent *gîtes*, which could sleep a total of sixteen people. Admittedly, it was all a bit minimal; space was extremely limited in the bedrooms, and we felt the combined shower-rooms/WCs not great for six people sharing, but it was an amazing feat nevertheless. The *gîte* at La Clède has two double beds, two single beds and a double futon sofa, but our preference in bookings was for two couples only. The house was ideal for this with its two bathrooms.

We felt rather foolish – like amateurs – when we explained this to them. I could tell Mike's brain was busying itself, probably not for the first time, about how simple it would be to split the house into two apartments, how we could make another entrance round the back, etc, etc.

"I think we should stick with quality, not quantity, Mike," I said, trying to justify our status quo to him. "Let's not even think about it. Ours is a different market. And I don't want to change the house that much anyway – it is half Ian's. Space is good."

Last year, forty-five per cent of our bookings were re-bookings. We wonder what Harold and Barbara's statistics are.

Gruesome news awaited us on our return. Lucky the kitten had caught her leg in an (illegal) trap, probably put out for rabbits. It had gone gangrenous and Roberte had paid the vet's bill to have it amputated. Vladia and Orane were distraught, and it prompted more anti-hunting arguments with their father, who certainly wouldn't have paid out for the operation. The girls could hardly bear to look at Lucky, wrapped up in her bandages and looking so pathetic and confused at what had happened to her. I tried to console them, and we all tried to comfort her.

"Elle apprendra à se débrouiller, à s'adapter. Elle fera sensation avec ses trois pattes, vous verrrez. On peut tous l'aider" (She'll learn to manage. She'll be a sensation with her three legs, you'll see. We can all help her out.)

They weren't convinced, but with time Lucky grew stronger and learned to get about very well despite her handicap. In fact, she's still an expert hunter and regularly chases and kills baby rabbits. One of the saddest things to watch, though, was (still is) when she wanted to scratch behind her right ear. Her head would turn and her little stump would wiggle. Whether she psychologically felt some relief, we don't know, but we'd rush over and scratch behind her ear anyway.

Now, if you're of a delicate disposition, don't read the next bit, as it's all about *la merde* (shit)! The *gîte's* septic tank was installed in 1969. Thirty years later, Mike and I agreed that it must surely be full up. If you know nothing about septic tanks, I'd like to sing their praises. For a start, you're responsible for your own waste, which is a great leveller! Your responsibility doesn't end at the U-bend, after which it's someone else's problem – an important lesson on the learning curve of life, metaphorically speaking! People living in large numbers in towns obviously need to have mains drains and sewage treatment centres. In the country, however, where density of population is much less, septic tanks work perfectly well. There are products to put down to increase the bacterial activity and decomposition, and as ours always has a rest over the winter months, it works a treat. In fact, in a discussion with the owner of a plumbers' merchant in Aubenas one day, we were told that, in theory, the liquid coming out of the tank is drinkable if the tank's working properly, though I don't know anyone personally who's put this theory to the test!

It is rumoured that, according to one of those Eurodirectives, France intends to have the whole country on mains drains within the next decade – in your dreams! – and that all septic tanks by law will have to be emptied and given a certificate every three years. If this isn't a ploy to create jobs, I don't know what is. And in a small commune like Ribes, with only 230 permanent residents, it's entirely unnecessary at the moment. The cost of laying main drains will be astronomical and will mean an increase in the rates, and every household will have to finance the routing of pipes from their property to join up with the mains. Unfortunately, this process has already started here because of a dispute between neighbours which couldn't be resolved. One neighbour's outflow, although 'clean', was running into another neighbour's land and he didn't like it – a classic clash between countryman and 'townie'. No amicable or legal solution could be found, so the regional water board decreed that both parties, and indeed the whole hamlet, Ribette, should go to the trouble and expense of putting mains drains in, which would 'in the year 200?' eventually flow into the future main sewage treatment plant (until then there's to be a small temporary one). When will this grand plan happen? Even the mayor shrugs and smiles!

But it was time to empty our tank, which because it dated from the sixties was built in cement and stood in the corner of one of the cellars, unburied. Its lid was a round cement disc, which had been cemented in place to seal it. Mike attacked it with his angle grinder – I stood by with pegs for our noses! What greater love hath a man who will open up your septic tank for you? God bless him. And I thought scrubbing tiles with sulphuric acid was bad! He managed to get it off. It was full, and there were two condoms lying on top of the pile of waste! Whose, we wondered, of course? Now what? As usual, when I have a local problem, I ask Christian the best way to deal with it. There are companies in the Yellow

Pages that offer an emptying service but they were quoting 2,000FF or more. I knew Christian wouldn't pay that and I was right. He knew a man who did. I called him, Alain from Joyeuse. Yes, he would come with his tractor and trailer at 10am the next day. Christian assured me that he would only charge 500FF.

He arrived on time and was very pleasant and professional in his working blues. He donned rubber gloves, inserted a large diameter flexible tube into our *fosse* and started pumping out the contents into a tank on his trailer. Afterwards, he flushed and scrubbed it out with clean water. (It seemed a shame to start soiling it again!) The whole thing took about three quarters of an hour. I had a bucket containing water and disinfectant for a hand wash and a cold beer waiting for him and he was very appreciative. He wrote me out a bill – 500FF – and I paid him in cash, asking if that was OK. (No VAT – another job on the black.)

"*Non, ça va très bien, merci.*"

"*Mais, ça a été vite fait. C'est moi qui dois vous remercier. Je vous appelle la prochaine fois?*" (That was a quick job. Thanks so much. Can I call you again next time?)

"*Oui, bien sûr. Allez, à la prochaine fois, alors. Au revoir.*"

And with that he picked up his scrubbing broom and left. We didn't see the point in making another appointment for 2029!

Mike and I looked at each other and grinned.

"That was brilliant. What a service," said Mike.

"Fifty quid's not much for doing that. Should I have given him a tip, do you think? I'll ask Christian."

When he came home from the bank that evening, I thanked him for his contact and said how impressed we'd been with him, that I'd given him a beer and should I have given him more than 500FF.

"*Non,*" he said. "*Je lui ai dit de vous faire le même prix qu'à moi.*" (I told him to charge the same price I pay)

"*Et qu'est-ce qu'il fait avec toute cette merde?*" I asked. (What does he do with it?)

"*Il la met dans ses vignes.*" (It goes on his vineyards)

"*Ah, ce sera une bonne année pour lui, alors*" (He'll have a good year then!)

"Oui, ce n'est pas mauvais, son vin." (His wine's not bad)

Of course, that's what they used to do with all the night soil. Until the middle classes invented Health and Safety Officers!

Mike's daughters came to visit us during the summer. Clare with her current beau, Jim, in June, Louise and her partner, Lawrence, and then Lauren[*], on a flying visit from Australia with Wayne, in July. This meant lots of play breaks in between bouts of work on the house for us – a good mix, which we hope prevented us from becoming 'dull boys'. We seemed to eat and drink quite frequently, inspired by all the wonderful produce in the markets – they were all keen to try out local delicacies and weren't difficult to feed (though both Louise and Clare were vegetarian, which can be a big problem if you're dependent on restaurants in France, as it's not considered socially acceptable!) We walked regularly in the forests that surround the village – there are two paleolithic burial sites higher up the mountain – stone coffins, carved out of the rock, one a single, one double. For the head tribesman and his consort, perhaps? Even the experts can't properly date them or say much about them, according to the information panels at the sites. These are great photo opportunity places, and everyone lies in them to have their picture taken, though most can't lie flat – people were quite a bit smaller in those far-off days.

We lazed around sunning, chatting or reading in the garden and at the beach. Our favourite time to go swimming *à poil* (naked) is around 8.30 in the morning, just as the sun is coming over the mountain ridge, so it's warm to dry off afterwards, and easier to go in initially! There's hardly ever anyone else there until around eleven, so you have paradise all to yourself. Time to do some nature watching and rock collecting, if you tire of sun worshipping. There's not the same pressure to 'do' on a holiday when it's family staying and they're likely to come back. Nevertheless, we did our fair share of sightseeing too. More of those medieval villages, like Largentière and its towering castle, Balazuc and Labeaume in the Ardèche river gorges, with their Romanesque churches, shady squares, narrow, cobbled streets and tiny houses

---

[*] Mike has a daughter Lauren and a son Stefan from a former relationship.

built right into and on to the rock. And there's always a river handy if it gets too hot. Banne boasts two lovely churches and the remains of a *château* at the top of the mountain. This has an extensive view over the surrounding countryside lying at its feet, which is a mix of scrubland bushes and limestone rocks that have been eroded into strange shapes over aeons of time. Bannes castle was ransacked during the Revolution and its owners beheaded in nearby Les Vans. Now summer concerts are held in the huge cellar which is all that's left intact. There's something quite unbeatable about live music on a warm, balmy night under the stars. It's something we Brits can't get very used to, as we pack blankets, thermoses and umbrellas for similar events! I have a fanciful theory that that's why we have a reputation for being so stoic and stalwart, because we've all been weaned on the disappointment of outings and picnics ruined or cancelled because of the weather. Weather does affect character, of course, and the warmer it gets, the more *joie de vivre* sets in and thrives.

The Pont d'Arc (a vast natural rock bridge spanning the Ardèche river), the best known landmark, and the thirty odd kilometers of gorges are must-sees for any first-time visitor, though there are nearly always too many tourists unless you go very early or late in the day. You have to bear with the approach to these natural wonders, though, as it's not such a pretty sight. When the potential for tourism was first realised, based around this magnificent part of the river, campsites and canoe hire stations arrived wholesale, like the Gold Rush on the west coast of America. The long stretch of road from Vallon to the start of the gorges has become a zoo and has this same American feel, with its endless hoardings advertising campsite after site, canoe and kayak hire, fast food restaurants, ranches, discos and the like – a complete sell-out. It's paid off in economic terms for the locals, as hundreds of thousands of people come every summer to camp and canoe on the river. On the quality side, however, it's a definite thumbsdown, and I gloomily fear it will only get worse. Unless something radical changes – does it ever? – they will overmilk the golden cow, bleed the river dry or let it get so polluted it's unfit to swim in or canoe on. Only then will they realise, as the wise Cree

Indian Chief has told us all, "that they cannot eat money". Unfortunately, it would seem that they cannot think beyond filthy lucre. Of course! They can **charge** people to visit the gorges, which is what's rumoured will happen – it might put some of the campers off. There are plans afoot for a huge theme park. Oh no!

If you can't bear what you see above ground and want to get away from this contemporary human madness, there are plenty of caves underground, with their natural, but fantastic stalactite/stalagmite formations. The lighting has been well designed and the effects are truly dramatic. Even more awesome are the incredible cave paintings of mammoth, bison, bear and other prehistoric animals, that were discovered in 1994 at La Grotte de Chauvet – over 30,000 years old, the oldest, it is claimed, though there is now some academic dispute about this date. The caves aren't open to the public. France learnt a hard lesson at Lascaux, where the effects of visitors gradually destroyed the paintings. But there's an exhibition centre at Vallon and a wonderful film of the archaeologists discovering the internal caverns. It makes the hairs on the back of my neck stand on end every time I see it.

Back on the surface again, these same people's pagan descendants were probably responsible for the dolmens that appear throughout the region. We went on one futile search with Louise and Lawrence on the plateau, after we'd 'done' the Gorges, but eventually found some nearer home in between Lablachère and St Alban-Auriolles. They all stand on the hillside, a short climb from the riverbed, which when we visited was almost dry with just a few frog-filled pools of stagnating water left. Formed by natural rain and river erosion into the soft chalk rock, these pools actually look almost man-made, with their rushes and reeds stylishly placed, as if landscape gardeners had been at work. Do your senses make you imagine it, or is there still something special and magical about these places? I think my vote's definitely for prehistoric, or Cro-Magnon, rather than modern man!

Talking of prehistoric man, our neighbour to the east is Jean Pansier, who's been around ever since most people can remember and hasn't appeared to age a day (he's actually nearing seventy-eight). Not much can be said about **his** creations; he hasn't made any, apart from peasant-type repairs to the doors, gutters and roofs still in use in his extremely large property, he being too occupied keeping body and soul together on the land. What parts of the building are no longer in use have gradually fallen into complete disrepair, and more than half of this lovely building (date of 1751 above one doorway) is empty, windowless and rotting. He does have one magnificent creation, though, and that is his large *potager* (vegetable patch), beautifully laid out and tended and containing every vegetable you can think of.

He also, until 1999, kept chickens. At night they would be shut inside his gated courtyard. Every morning, he would open his gates and shoo the chickens out to do the rounds of the hamlet, picking and pecking in everyone else's gardens and *potagers*, but unable to get into his, surrounded as it was by a sturdyish, though much repaired, fence. As you can imagine, this rather unneighbourly act didn't go down very well with anyone trying to grow anything – six or seven hungry hens can do a fair bit of damage to plants. It drove my mother crazy, and my father. Ribes legend has it that he once knocked one dead with a golf ball! Alan, now hero of the hamlet, used to practise his swing in the courtyard.

People would complain mildly and ask Jean repeatedly to keep his chickens penned in. He would just shrug. Chickens were women's work, and he lived with a fragile wife we never saw and his handicapped (Down's Syndrome) sister, Josette (who also looked after the rabbits and could be seen daily, walking around brandishing a sickle as she collected greenery for them). So not much chance of getting them on our side. Over the years, other neighbours tried running the birds over, hitting them with whatever came to hand; one once got so mad, he picked a chicken up and broke its neck. Mike managed to get hold of one one day, carried it by its feet to Jean's *potager* and dropped it in there over the fence. But the hint wasn't taken; still those chickens kept on coming. If we were in, we'd chase them away; if we weren't, anything growing was up for grabs. We didn't have or want any gates or fences to keep them out of our courtyard and we couldn't barricade every one of our garden terraces. We have quite a long perimeter. If we were visited by boar, it would be quite a different matter. We're really talking damage with boar.

We'd just put in seven rhubarb plants. We went out shopping. When we got back, they weren't there any more.

"Right, that's it," Mike and I said in unison. "It's them or us."

Next time they all appeared, we confused them. Instead of the usual rushing and shooing they'd come to expect, they heard encouraging, cooing noises from me.

"Here, little chuck-chucks, come here to mama, come on". Mike, meanwhile, was waiting in the cellar with a large fishing net (nephew Tom's, I think). I gradually won their confidence and managed to steer two of them towards, and in through, the cellar door and shut it. A great deal of banging and squawking followed. Several minutes later, Mike appeared triumphant, a few bloody scratches on his arms and a pillow case in each hand containing two now docile chickens.

"That wasn't as easy as I thought it would be," he said. "They didn't half put up a fight. Right, where shall we take them?"

"The other side of the river. They can't fly far or swim, so I think that should do it."

Mike's wounds dressed, we got in the van, drove to the bottom of the valley and deposited them near an isolated house on the far bank.

"They'll probably go there for food and get adopted, don't you think?" Mike asked me. "Either that, or a fox'll get them. Tough. Two down, four to go."

This less than simple operation was repeated twice more. Josette could later be seen wandering around, looking and calling out for the Pansier chickens. She wouldn't see them again. I didn't think I was a good enough actress to ask her what had happened to them! We thought they'd be replaced, but no new chickens appeared. We'd kidnapped and won.

Now we were chicken-free, we thought we could take a short holiday. We were on a high anyway, exhilarated by our anarchic deeds! We decided to go west and explore the valley of the Tarn. We particularly like mountains and rivers, and France has these in abundance. It really is such an amazing country, with so many different landscapes and cultures to explore and experience – the

States in miniature – with a bit more history! You can do and see a lot in four or five days away and get a complete break from home life. We spend a while on research with maps and guide-books. Then we organise the van.

A van is a truly wonderful vehicle. Not only does it hold lots of stuff, from bits of furniture to bags of cement; it also doubles as a camping car. Mike's van is already full of shelves and cubby holes to store all his stocks of washers and widgets and things, so it's simply a case of taking most of these out and replacing them with water containers, gas light and cooker – all the necessary camping paraphernalia – putting in our 1.20m mattress down the middle, and it/we are ready to go. He's even designed and made an ingen-ious roll-up awning with plastic plumbing pipe and tarpaulins, so we've got a covered, outside space as well, if the weather's not on our side. We're free to travel as the mood and places of interest take us.

If we feel like a bit more comfort, we'll stay in an *auberge* (around 250FF for a room – in Britain this would be prohibitive); otherwise, we're more than happy in a campsite @ 50FF. Out of high season, finding places to stay over without having to book in advance is not usually a problem. *Camping sauvage* (that is, not in a camp site) is forbidden by law in most communes, but we have been known, when we're miles from civilisation, to drive into a forest or follow some barely driveable path to a lovely wild spot and just park and overnight there. We're very clean campers – you wouldn't know we'd been through. We "plug up our hole." *

Now that the *gîte* had a 'reborn' *fosse*, our own lack of one was a major cause for concern. We simply couldn't carry on with the existing system, especially now that there were two of us. We had

---

* Reference to a section in Ben Elton's *Stark* (Sphere Books Ltd, 1989), entitled 'The Desert Oak', which tells how aborigines on walkabout in the desert would drink from this tree with its huge capacity to store water. They would cut a hole in the trunk and lie under it open-mouthed to catch the drips. When they'd drunk their fill, they wouldn't just leave it to drip, but plugged the hole with gum from the gum tree, so that the next guy could do likewise. This tale should be compulsory reading/listening for all human beings from the cradle on.

to install one, and our cellar offered a suitable site for the tank – like the concrete one in the other cellar, only these days *fosses* are lighter and made in plastic. You see, that's something else you can get into a van – a 1,000 litre tank! – and all the plumbing accessories. First of all, we had to build a sturdy platform for it to stand on. It needed height to get the necessary fall into the existing drains. (It **is** very sturdy, but, even now, every time I look at it, I cannot stop my mind visualising the platform collapsing, the tank falling ... !)

Inside *chez nous*, we also had to make changes to the 'biggest loo in the world', as it severely limited the number and kind of people we could ask to stay. Imagine everybody sharing a loo with no walls and no door! We spent hours trying to plan alternatives. Building a proper, enclosed *cabinet de toilette* meant partition walls, which seemed unsuitable in this large mezzanine space with its high, pitched ceiling and exposed roof timbers. It also housed two single beds, but walls would necessitate changing the staircase – a spiral one instead of a ladder type? In practice, spirals take up even more space. We just couldn't come up with a good solution, so in the end we left it wall-less. Instead, we built high divisions of shelving units, backed with insulation board, around the toilet area, where we added a small washbasin, bathroom accessories and a screen door. It was extremely cheap and simple and gave us the added benefit of more storage. It meant that ablutions could be carried out in reasonable privacy, though it's still far from ideal. This is what our poor friends have to put up with. They all receive a 'health warning', but there's no room for anally retentive folk here!

In our bedroom, which does have solid walls and a door, we put in another loo for our own use (and for anyone who does need more privacy!) Mike and I feel intimate enough with each other to be able to handle this, though such an extremely *en suite* arrangement is not to everyone's taste, judging from some of the shock/horror reactions from people taking a look round! All these new mod-cons meant large-scale plumbing changes down in the cellar, which involved poor Mike in crawling around on his stomach on top of a pile of rubble inside the 'room' under our terrace, in a space no higher than a couple of feet. This had been a dumping ground for leftover rubble when Geo and Serge were knocking down buildings, making new terraces and so on for my parents. Pipes inside the cellar had to be connected to go through the septic tank, and outside to go into drains to the existing soakaway. We also needed vent pipes from both tanks to go high up above the rooftops. I'm sure none of our neighbours have these, though they are required by law. Unfortunately, if the wind's in the wrong direction, you occasionally get a whiff – it's just like a giant fart and then, thankfully, goes away quickly. Not for nothing was 1999 called the Year of the Bogs!

The *gîte* was free by this time, mid-September, so that two sets of friends who came to visit didn't have to put the friendship to the test in the 'bogs department'; they could stay comfortably and in a more civilised fashion next door! Trish was a friend of Mike's; she and her husband, who had recently died, had been clients of his. She was having a tough time coming to terms with being on her own again and was becoming increasingly unhappy with her life in Whitstable. Visiting us in Ribes was her first time of travelling abroad alone, so it was a brave thing to do in the circumstances. She was a pushover for France and our life style – fell for it hook, line and sinker, has since sold up and now lives in a small village not far from Poitiers.

John and Mavis turned up in their gleaming green, newly renovated VW Beetle, sniffed the air and looked at the holes and pipes in the ground.

"Bad time to arrive, is it? What's up, Mike? Looks like a drains problem," asked John, who was familiar with such things, owning as he did an extremely successful Whitstable builders' merchants.

"Had one, John. The worst's over, thank goodness," said Mike, emerging from his hole.

"Yes. Good timing, actually," I said, welcoming them both. "Let's stop now. We've only got the filling in to do. Come up and have a drink."

Time to play again – more sightseeing. Best trip with these two was to the famous Pont du Gard, which none of us had seen. It was a most beautiful day, sunny but not too hot – a lovely drive down there and a picnic in the almost empty carpark, on giant stones in the cool shade of plane trees. This was before the new Visitor Centre was built, and apart from a café and small souvenir shop, that was all there was. It was very surreal. Out in the wilds and you suddenly come upon this huge, spectacular, perfect construction – 49m high, 275m long, with 52 arches – over the Gardon river, built to supply water to Roman Nîmes. You have to hand it to them. "Yes, very clean, those Romans. Always washing themselves they were."*

One of our best days out with Trish started with Les Vans market, our favourite. It's not too big a town, and it has a brilliant social mix, including artists and writers – *les intellos* – north African and African immigrants, and, as well as your normal range of folk from farmers to exquisitely dressed and coiffed *bourgeoisie,* a healthy dollop of *marginaux.* In the sixties many dropouts came here from Paris and elsewhere to lead an alternative life – mainly because property was so cheap – and some of them and their descendants are still there. Mike and I once saw an entire family – mum, dad and three kids – all dressed in home-made suede and fur like North American Indians! (Needless to say, the children were all beautifully behaved!) The feel is pretty 'laid back', therefore, rather than the hustle and bustle of Aubenas (the same distance from Joyeuse in the other direction), where people seem somewhat more concerned with the rat race and climbing the social ladder. In Les Vans there are bars all around the central square where you can sit and watch them all!**

An extremely pleasant morning doing just that and making the odd food purchase was followed by a picnic on the banks of the Chassezac river, and a visit to Thines. This is an extremely old and isolated mountain village, famous now for its 12th century church and its monument to the *maquisards*. During the last war, the

---

* Tony Hancock talking to Huw Lloyd at the end of *The Blood Donor* from *Hancock's Half Hour* by Ray Dalton and Alan Simpson (BBC Publications, 1974)

** The distinction lies in the quality of the café society - whether it's the Jean-Paul Sartre/Simone de Beauvoir ("I think, therefore I am") arty kind, or the urban professional and dysfunctional youth kind!

French Resistance would hole up here, to hide from the Gestapo. The whole area is so wild and inaccessible, it was considered the perfect place. It wasn't for two of them, who were tracked down and, with several of the adult males from the village, were shot and pushed over the mountain top. Notre Dame de Thines is described as an "exceptional jewel of Romanesque art". *Polychrome* (multicoloured), built in grey granite, dark schist and red sandstone, its interior is beautifully decorated with sculptures and carvings. The naïve wooden sculpture of the Mother and Child was especially beautiful. (I saw it long ago on a visit with my parents. But it was stolen in 1973 and still hasn't been recovered.) You certainly go back in time walking around the village. Today, only a handful of near self-sufficient families still lives there – off the land and their skills as artisans. And tourism, of course, though coach parties are thankfully kept to a minimum, since one has to walk the last kilometre.

In early October, we went off on another mini-holiday. It's the best and only time for us to do this. We don't like to go away when we've got guests staying. But when our season's over, and we feel we've earned it – and elsewhere, too, most tourists have gone home – it's quiet and infinitely more pleasant getting out and about. Still just warm enough, though, to camp out if we want or need to. We were keen to explore the towns, villages and wildlife (wolves and vultures) of the Lozère, one of the least spoiled *départements* in France, and beyond. Fabulous places we'd heard of and read about – Conques, Rocamadour (Mike had already visited), Cordes sur Ciel, Albi, Carcassonne, Béziers, more Roman culture at Oppidum d'Ensérune and down to the Med at Sète, to meet up with friends with a boat moored there. A fantastic trip!

During our last few weeks in Ribes, we busied ourselves with the endless house maintenance, painting shutters, doors and windows, checking the roof tiles and the party wall joins, to help it survive the winter. As the weather cooled, we moved inside to do some plastering and painting work in our *salle de séjour*, making it all look a lot cleaner and more civilised. By the second week in November, it was getting very chilly at night. Our tenants in Canterbury would soon be vacating, and it was time to stock up with wine and drive home for the winter. But winter hit us with a vengeance sooner than we thought.

We left Ribes in lovely warm sunshine and started our climb up through the Beaume valley. Just south of Valgorge, we saw threatening dark clouds appearing over the mountain. At Loubaresse, it started snowing heavily. But it was too late to turn back. And Mike likes a challenge! The snow was virgin and deep on the plateau. We had no chains, and it was almost impossible to drive round the bends, because of the freezing ice and lack of tarmac on which to grip. We passed only one vehicle throughout the entire nightmarish journey, which took us well over double the normal time. If anything had happened to us or the van – white vans don't stand out well in a snowdrift! – it would have been quite a while before we were discovered. The snow and sleet continued throughout the drive north. Mike, who knew the Bedford more intimately than I, opted to drive most of the way and by nightfall he was exhausted. We fell into bed in our familiar, friendly hotel in Montargis. By five o'clock next day we were back in Blightey, safe and sound, with lots of news of an extremely varied and busy year to relate to friends and family.

Our winter life passed pleasantly enough in Canterbury. We both worked part-time, Mike helping favourite clients with any problems or new projects in their various houses. I'd go along too when I wasn't working with Alistair, a freelance journalist, another of Mike's clients, for whom I did some research and sub-editing. He was then in the process of launching a business newsletter called *Ethical Performance,* all about corporate social responsibility, the latest PR thing for businesses. In essence, it means that companies, as well as making a Profit, should also consider People and the Planet.

We binged out on culture as always – there are great cinemas and theatres on the university campus. Even English TV is pretty good when you know you'll only watch it for a few months! We walked a lot, especially with the Bromley Ramblers, friends of brother Ian and Tina, with pub lunches afterwards. We travelled around like gypsies visiting friends and relatives and spent the New Millennium night in Devon with our friend, Lovely Rita.

DO YOU TIP THE DUNNY MAN?

She'd been a neighbour in Canterbury and escaped to Devon to join up with Richard, leaving her stressful job as Tourist Manager. I think our dropping-out life may have played a small part in her decision! It absolutely poured down on 31 December 1999 and we never made it to the firework display in Bideford!

- 6 -
A MAN'S HOME IS HIS CASTLE (2000)

BY THE BEGINNING of April, Mike was desperate to get back to France. He was becoming as passionate about life there as I was. So we went into life-change mode, at which we were getting rather good, I have to say. This involves spring-cleaning the Canterbury house (and that means every nook and cranny), prior to letting; packing all our personal stuff into the loft, and things destined to go with us to Ribes into the porch, prior to van-packing; booking the ferry (who's offering the best deal this year?), sorting the finances; and informing authorities, like the Council and the utilities of our move, not as easy as you might imagine. The mail redirection is always a hassle. Royal Mail hardly ever gets things right, sending me other people's mail, losing letters, ignoring dates of contracts, just to mention some regular cock-ups. They really couldn't run a bath!

And one of the worst headaches is – was – trying to get car insurance in Britain if you're planning to be out of the country for more than ninety days. Last year, we'd finally blown a fuse on being told by a 'senior risk assessor' in Norwich Union head office, that I should drive my Renault 5 the 850 odd kilometres back from the Ardèche, take a day return across the Channel and drive back, (all "on the wrong side of the road", as they see it), rather than have an endorsement put in the policy. I was fifty years of age, had been driving for thirty years and only once been in an accident when something – a piece of debris in a motorway lane – hit me! So I'd registered my car in France, paid one third of the premium, no tax, and needed a *contrôle technique* (MOT) only every two years. I could also drive anywhere in Europe when I liked, for as long as I liked! Mike planned to do likewise when we eventually traded in the Bedford.

A MAN'S HOME IS HIS CASTLE (2000)

Once again in this dependable old vehicle, loaded to the gunnels, we arrived in Ribes mid April and were greeted enthusiastically by our neighbours opposite. Roberte and Orane, sitting in late afternoon sunshine on their terrace and starting on their *bronzage* (tans), had spotted us coming up the *calade* (steep hill) and had leapt to their feet waving. What better welcome could you have! Lilac and roses were in full bloom together, as always, around the courtyard. A red climbing rose, which we'd started to train over the *tonnelle* covering the terrace last year, was also out in profusion. Kisses and hugs from beautiful women, sighs of contentment (especially from Mike), but from both of us. Home again. Time to unpack. They couldn't believe what Mike had managed to cram into the van. He has an expert left-side of brain, spatial awareness facility! Very useful indeed.

Over the next few days we were absorbed as usual in getting the house and garden into some sort of shape, in preparation for another season. In the process of phoning round to let people know we were back, our German friend, Gunhi (short for Gunhilde) asked us if we had some free time to make her a pergola. We'd constructed several for vines to grow over at our mutual friends, Jeff and Renée's place, and she'd also liked ours at the back of the *gîte*. She had a spot in her garden just below the house where she'd planted a couple of kiwis and wanted a paved, shady place to sit. So, Pergolas R Us went into action! After three days, her freshly sprouting kiwi vines had their new support and we had another happy customer!

April and May are wonderful months for working outside, as it's not yet too hot, and heavy jobs like digging are possible as the ground is still damp and friable – in summer it sets like cement and has to be hoed before watering. We dug to increase the size of our vegetable patch. We especially wanted to grow lots of tomatoes, as we both adore them, and they flourish here bathed in so much sunshine. Anyone from northern climes who has only tasted supermarket tomatoes (and other fruit) hasn't lived. The deep red colour and the flavour! Sliced and spread with a little *tapenade* (a kind of vegetarian *pâté* made with olives and anchovies), they are divine!

Many of the villagers have huge patches and grow all the veg-etables and salads they'll need throughout the seasons. But tending them is very labour-intensive and as tying as pets. We were more than happy to limit our own produce to salads, cucumbers, beans and tomatoes. It's not at all economical, as when things are in season, they're very cheap in the shops; everybody else has them and you can hardly give them away. It is a real joy, though, just to walk into the garden and pick a few things to put on the plates for the next meal. We had to fence it against marauding rabbits. Lucky just wasn't catching enough of them!

My cat-loving journalist friend, Marianne, who was covering the Cannes Film Festival and then doing some teaching at a film school in Avignon, came to spend a few jolly days with us afterwards. It was her first visit to La Clède, and it must have been quite warm as we have pictures of us all by the river. Louise and Lawrence visited with their friends, Paul and Suzanne – staying in the *gîte*, as we weren't posh enough yet our side. We have it on good authority that these friends' baby son George was conceived in the Blue Room! An additional pleasure was that some of our favourite guests were returning for the second or third time, so it was like having friends next door for a while.

We had entertainment over the road. The Balazuc Brothers – sounds like a circus act – were tiling the terrace. There'd been a big pile of tiles in their cellar porch for as long as I could remember, and Roberte had been nagging Christian for some time to get on with it. He and his three brothers, Alain and twins, Eric and Joël, who don't look remotely alike, had obviously at last found 'windows' in their busy schedules. It took them over a week and they weren't lucky with the weather, as it poured down just after they'd finished the cementing, and again after the grouting. The terrace and steps didn't half look good, though, and made our patchy concrete ramp look a bit sick! We promised to tile it to match later in the year! Meanwhile, as the temperature rose, we were busy making shutters for all the windows – six in all – on our side.

The Balazuc family (Christian's grandfather, Maurius and his wife Yvonne) had taken in a young Belgian, Leopold, sixteen years of age, who had arrived in Ribes in 1940, as part of the exodus fleeing from the Germans during the war. Geo was then thirteen. Thirty years later, Leo returned to Ribes. Geo was now married to Jeanine from nearby Lablachère, who'd never met Leo but had heard family tales about him. She was the first person he saw when he came back to the house and she had immediately said, "You must be Leopold." He was very touched by this, and a profound friendship developed between the two families, which continues to this day. Leopold, or Pol, as he came to be called, was given a small piece of their land, on which to put a caravan, and the parents, children and grandchildren visit every summer. We've got to know *Les Belges* too – they're extremely kind and warm people – and it's become a kind of tradition now for all of us to go to the river beach one evening and have a bathe and a picnic. It's also an excellent opportunity for Mike to dazzle them all with his *pâtisserie* skills, and, in fact, Pol's wife Berthe proposed to him after sampling his apple cake!

The big heat arrived and our bedroom on the first floor was getting hotter and hotter, despite the shutters, but we had no choice but to sleep there. Apart from the kitchen downstairs, it was the only 'clean' part of the house. We'd started *un grand chantier* (major building works) in the mezzanine and the *salle de séjour* (lounge) below, which went on for weeks. The first part of it was an especially difficult and dirty job, cleaning and finishing the upper stone walls, the highest of which, the one behind the chimneybreast, was eight metres (to the ridge). I'd already cleaned and pointed about a quarter of this wall (to first floor level) years before, and we'd slurried and painted all the other lounge walls last year. These were all covered to protect them against what was about to shower down on them.

It was a pretty amazing circus act of our own, though no-one was watching us. Both armed with wire brushes and wearing masks and nothing else, we worked perched atop some rather Heath Robinson, home-made scaffolding. This comprised two high ladders, that Mike had tied off for safety, with a strong, thick plank between acting as a working platform. We were attempting to clean decades of soot from chestnut-drying fires and carbon caused by the house fire off the stones. Not a nice job. We coughed and spluttered our way through it and got very, very dirty. Black sludge in the shower afterwards. The next stage was cleaner though just as difficult, heaving buckets of cement up to working level to point the stones, now free of soot but still very dark.

Mike had another idea when we were half way down the wall. There were several holes in it where the ends of the old beams that supported the chestnut grille had been set. He thought it would be a nice idea to fill these with paler stones as a reminder of what the space had been used for before. It would, anyway, have been difficult to find black stones locally to match, necessitating a trip to Jaujac in the Ardèche valley, one of the few places in France with basalt rock. And, odd as it may seem, it was hard enough to find stones to fit anyway. We made numbered templates of the holes and took them to the river to match them up. It sort of worked, but a lot of them didn't seem to fit well when we got them back! Finishing that wall was a slow, painstaking business, but the end result was brilliant.

We found a pleasing – and quicker and easier – way to finish the other upstairs stone walls, otherwise we'd have been at it for months. We painted them over with a cement slurry of thick custard consistency, so that the joints were filled in, the dirty stones were covered, but their shapes were still visible. Some of the unremovable soot at the fire end came through as brown blotches, but it all added to the overall effect. We rationalised that, as the fire was part of the building's history, this justified it – quite some rationalisation, I know, but in fact the look of the space once finished added weight to our argument. It resembled the inside of a medieval castle. Interior designers doing Dungeon and Dragons or Harry Potter themed bedrooms for kids would have charged at least £10,000 for this effect! And when we'd finished that, we sprayed all the walls with a diluted Unibond mixture to 'set' the finish and cut down on future dust – another from Mike's repertoire of ideas. To finish upstairs, we painted the ceiling white and stained the wooden floor and beams chestnut.

Downstairs in the lounge, the flagstone floor and the chimney-breast were next on the *'relooking'* (makeover) list. There were several cracked and uneven flagstones and there was something not quite right with the chimneybreast. We sat and stared at it. "I like the bit above the mantlepiece; the asymetrical shape's good," I volunteered. Mike continued: "It's the bottom bit that's wrong; the vertical sides aren't thick enough. We need to make it look more solid."

Amazing Building Product No 4: Ciporex. This is the cement equivalent of MDF – a white powder that's been glued and compressed into lightweight building blocks of all sizes and thicknesses. You cut them with a saw to the size you want. So, we did, cementing them on to the insides of the existing walls of the chimneybreast, and then slurrying the whole lot over with white cement to hide the joins. Several coats of white paint were needed to cover decades of dirt on the hood of the chimneybreast. The terracotta tiles, which made up the mantelpiece, cleaned up well, and we matched it with more – bargain – terracotta tiles on the floor. Result: *dix sur dix*. Moving flagstones is not an easy job either! Like an extremely heavy 3D jigsaw. Mike got stuck in, taking good stones from in front of the chimneybreast to replace the bad elsewhere, and filling in the resulting gap with cement, which we anticipated covering with a fireside rug. Pointing and sealing the flags finished the room.

The neighbours had been curious while we were doing this. They never saw us, as we spent every day working inside. On one occasion, I think we were downstairs sealing the flagstones, in the nude as usual, and the doorbell rang. Panic, where were our clothes? I luckily had a handy sarong, but Mike had nothing. He scuttled into the kitchen to hide. It was one of the second-homers in the hamlet, Anne Gaudemar, come to ask our opinion on covering their terrace, so I had to call Mike. He came out of the kitchen with an apron on! I couldn't stop laughing, as I explained that she'd caught us working *à poil* (naked) because of the heat, but I don't think she believed me!

Other neighbours were invited to inspect our handiwork, which they all agreed was *très bien fait*. Then an argument started up between them as to whether we should remove an old beam or not. It had been an original part of the construction of the chestnut grille and had survived the fire. Now it crossed the width of the room on its own, no longer supporting anything and we planned to cut it out (to use as a string in renovating the staircase). When we said this, some of the men, in particular Albert and Pierre (our neighbours behind), were horrified. We had to leave it; it was original, they said. We did remove it and when they came back again, they all agreed it looked better without it! I think Orane summed it up best:

"*Wowww! C'était tout noir avant ... et maintenant c'est tout blanc! Qu'il est beau, ce mur.*" (It was so dark, now it's so white. That wall's lovely.) I'd sat and stared at this end of the house so many times, picturing how it would be when it was finished. It was just as I'd dreamed it would look. We'd done it and it looked really great!

We showed it off to Clare when she visited, on her own this time. She'd come down on the train from Ashford to Lille, then Lille to Valence by TGV. It only took six hours. When Mike took her back in the van – it only had two seats – to Valence (before the new TGV station was open), they'd had time to have lunch and a brief look round the town before the train left. Mike had spotted a hardwood, octagonal, slatted garden tabletop, put out by some dustbins. Never one to look a gift horse in the mouth, he made a quick inspection of it. Not much wrong with it – one of the slats had warped and come adrift – which meant it was worth having. So he picked it up and carried it back to the van. Clare, apparently, was not remotely embarassed. She's used to her dad! It was a real good find. We made a base for it, stained the two to match and placed it on the stone circle (made with flat stones from the river) in the garden[*]. We had to have four new hardwood chairs to go with it, of course, and there were some *en promo* at Vedel's hardware store in Joyeuse. They came from some country in Asia, which is probably cutting down all its rainforests as I write. We're all hypocrites, aren't we? But at least we recycled the table!

In late September, we had a week's break in the *gîte*, and decid-

---

[*] As the table was larger than the one it replaced, we had to enlarge the stone circle. Every action seems to lead us on to another job to do!

ed we needed a holiday. We'd been working almost flat out for over two months. We both fancied going into Spain, and decided on the west coast, as I was especially keen to go see the Guggenheim Museum in Bilbao. We travelled through familiar countryside in the Lozère and Aveyron, ending up in the endless fields of maize and sunflowers in the Gers and camping near Auvillar, an attractive village on the Garonne. The next day our journey took us through the pine forests of *les Landes* and on into Biarritz. We found a near-empty campsite still open just south of it, then went back into town to explore.

It was a wild, wet, windy day with massive rollers hitting the sandy beach. The surfers were out in force – best surfing in Europe. What a surreal sight to watch them stripping out of their wetsuits in front of the elegant, five-star Hotel du Palais, one of the last great luxury hotels in France, according to our guide book – "The service and food are impeccable, the mood refreshingly unstuffy." How the other half lives. We walked around, stopping to press our noses on the shopfronts selling the likes of Versace jeans for over 3,000FF. This was some affluent place, and we were soon into one of our favourite pastimes, people-watching, over a drink or two in the numerous cafés on the front. The restaurant menus were all on the pricey side, but we eventually found a Belgian bar offering *Moules-Frites* for 55FF on its blackboard out-side.

The time was just after seven, a bit early to eat in France, but we went inside to a friendly welcome from a handsome young waiter, who showed us to a table near the window where we could watch the ocean as the light faded. Too cloudy for a sunset, unfortunately, so we turned our attention to the small group of businessmen seated at the bar having a post-work drink and telling stories. We ordered a couple of beers and MF for two, and wrote a few postcards while we waited. After about twenty min-utes, an enormous pot of *moules* arrived, and two portions of chips. I lifted the lid to smell the heavenly hot aroma of sea, wine, garlic and herbs. It was full to the brim.

"D'you think we'll manage this lot?" I asked Mike. He had a look inside. "Yes, no prob ..." A second pot was set on the table.

"Oh, good heavens, there's more!"

We ate non-stop for an hour; our jaws ached from eating! The best feast ever, but we needed to walk it off a bit. Outside, it was another wonderful world. The town lit up at night was a magical place, totally different from its daylight persona. We became more and more enchanted as we walked along the sea road, taking in exotic gardens *en route*, and stopping to stare out at the lighted causeway to the *Rocher de la Vierge* and listen to the crashing waves, hurling their foamy mass at the rocks.

"It's wonderful," I said. "We'll come back when we're rich and famous and eat at the Palais, eh?!" "Yes, OK. Shall we go back to our campsite now then?!"

And I have to say those mussels were quite an aphrodisiac! Mañana España.

We took the *autopista* through Basque country towards Bilbao. It certainly felt and looked like a different country; different road signs in two strange languages were confusing to start with. Big mountains with big tenement blocks and factories all over them. Bilbao is a large industrial, not particularly attractive city, but the Guggenheim was well signposted and not hard to find. It was a brilliant day of blue sky and sunshine, and suddenly there it was in front of us, like an oasis, a shining gold jewel surrounded by water. (It's actually covered in titanium 'tiles' which reflect everything around, especially the sun and the river.) We parked amazingly easily nearby and were drawn, as if magnetised, towards it. At the entrance is Jeff Koons' floral puppy standing over twelve metres high. The modern architecture of the museum itself you either love or hate; we both loved it, inside and out. It's the sexiest building I've ever seen! Such ingenuity in its design – it's actually got the existing road/bridge going right through it at one end!

Among the works on show inside, we were lucky enough to see some Picassos, Matisses and Rothcos – in the permanent collection. The modern art contents can cause the same extremes of emotion as the building, though what we saw was limited – several floors were out of bounds as new exhibitions were in the process of being constructed. Mike was particularly scathing about some of it, I remember, in particular Room 104, containing

Easter 1966: Peg and Al

Summer 1966: work in progress on the terrace extension after the henhouse had been demolished

La Clède in 1966, showing the property in the apex of our L-shaped house and our neighbour's original roofline

In 1969, our neighbour extended upwards, changing the roofline. 'La Bête du Gevaudan' has been a pain for over 30 years!

Jan and brother Ian at the launch of Lilac and Roses, The France Shop, Canterbury, March 2001

Mike and Malcolm working on the roof of La Clède, October 1995

Balazuc family tree

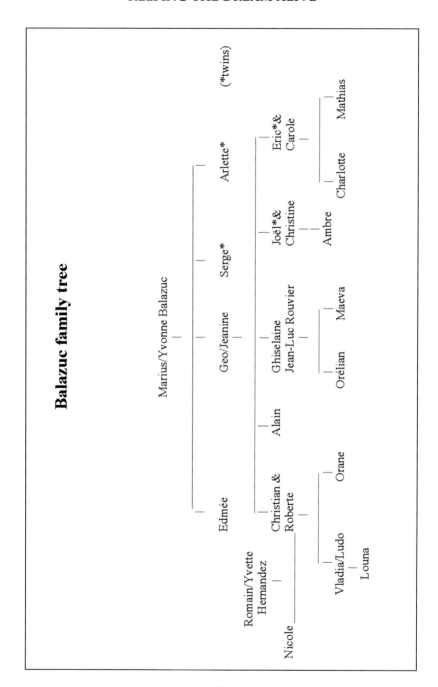

(*twins)

Marius/Yvonne Balazuc

Edmée   Geo/Jeanine   Serge*   Arlette*

Christian & Roberte   Alain   Ghiselaine Jean-Luc Rouvier   Joël*& Christine   Eric*& Carole

Romain/Yvette Hernandez

Orane   Orélian   Maeva   Ambre   Charlotte   Mathias

Nicole

Vladia/Ludo

Louna

Above: Three beautiful Balazucs: Roberte (behind), Charlotte (left) and Louna

Right: Christian with his new toy

Mike at Tom Simpson's memorial on Mt Ventoux

*Annual picnic with the Balazucs and 'les Belges' at a favourite
river beach*

Lucky as a kitten (note the heart patch)

La Clède - the Owl and the Pussycat

Wine-making at Issac (chez Jeff and Renée) with friend Patrick

'Punters' turned fab friends. L to R: Roger, (Mike), Trish, Tony and Gill, around the recycled garden table

several tall, round plywood 'mazes' and a sculpture of three upright, curved steel sheets, forming two 'corridors', all of which filled an entire gallery. "This isn't art," he snorted. "Some of it looks like basic carpentry to me."

"It's art, if it moves you in some way and because someone has created it" was my more tolerant, if somewhat patronising view!

"Any half-good builder with a hammer and a bag of nails could make that!"

"Ah, but he didn't. Richard Serra did and they're called Tourqued Ellipses and The Snake! They made you cross anyway! You were moved, so it's Art. I rest my case!" Whatever your opinion, the Guggenheim is a pretty fantastic place to spend a day in.

It might have been easy finding our goal. Getting out of Bilbao proved to be the complete opposite. We'd planned to go inland and cross the Pyrenees in Spain. We went round and round the town several times, trying to find a sign that matched a town on our map. We'd hit the same roundabout for the fifth time, having driven through some decidedly dodgy-looking quarters, even up what we thought was an exit road that took us high out above the city and then back down into it again! We were so frustrated by this time that we decided to abandon our plan and eventually found our way back on to the motorway heading towards France. By the time we reached Irun just before the border, we were hungry and determined to eat a good *paella* at least. But more disappointment and frustration was to come. We walked round and round Irun, like all the other Spaniards, (or should I say Basques to be more politically correct? And you need to be in Irun, it seems). They, though, were not looking for a restaurant, just doing their daily promenading and socialising prior to a meal around ten o'clock or even later. We asked in our faltering Spanish but the reception was very definitely unfriendly. We finally found a backstreet bar advertising *paella*. It was the worst one we'd ever eaten. I think it had been put by for the dogs, and we only managed a few forksful before leaving in disgust.

At the border there was a Spanish truckdrivers' strike going on, and we had to queue to cross the line. Pickets were out and stopping all lorries and vans, and we were pulled over and politely asked what we were carrying. *"Nada. Touristas inglés,"* we said and were waved through, somewhat frazzled and pleased to back on French soil. By now it was dark and too late to try and find a room and we decided we'd pull into an *aire d'autoroute* (motorway services) and park overnight. This is quite common practice for travellers, as opposed to *touristas*, as the ablution facilities are usually excellent with loos, showers, drinking water all on hand. We found a secluded spot away from the pumps and restaurant and settled down for the night. When we woke in the early morning we couldn't believe our eyes. We were surrounded on all sides by giant container lorries. None was being allowed through the border and they were backing up for many, many kilometres. We talked to one desperate Scot, a self-employed haulier, who'd been stuck there for two days, waiting to take his load south. He was powerless to do anything and losing money by the minute. We left him and the others behind and drove east towards the mountains, glad to be out of all the madness.

We certainly lucked out with our overnight spot the next evening. Just after Arudy, around dusk, we took a chance, on seeing a sign *Lac*, and drove up along a dirt track for a couple of kilometers before arriving at a truly delightful setting to spend the night. It was a fishing lake, complete with a couple of picnic tables and drinking water on tap! We had the place to ourselves and quickly prepared our picnic to be in time for the sunset. The camping gas came out to heat up one of our tinned ready-meals (these are good in France; no Heinz rubbish here) – a duck *cassoulet* (stew with beans), bread, a bottle of Merlot, salad, cheese and fruit. We felt like kings and enthusiastically planned our next-day trip higher (to over 3,000 metres) into the mountains – no trouble at all for the Bedford! It was not to be, however. We awoke to drizzly rain; the lake was barely visible through the mist, let alone any mountains! Quick change of plan. What do you do on a wet day in the Pyrenees? Go underground to a cave. Which is how we came to visit *"la merveille des Pyrénées"* – *les Grottes de Betharram*. My first cave experience, and it was marvellous.

To go to Lourdes, or not? The guidebook advised staying away if you weren't "led there by faith". Could it be as bad as rumour had it? I'm afraid it's so bad, you have to keep pushing your jaw back up! Such shocking sights. I'd seen Moslems crouching towards Mecca, Buddhists prostrating themselves before gigantic Buddhas, Hindus similarly before Shiva and Ganesh, but Europeans throwing themselves in front of statues of the Virgin Mary was a new shock for me. Similarly, I'd seen beggars in India, who'd mutilated themselves or their children, but these desperate, terribly deformed and handicapped people being wheeled along by their 'carers' in the special red, fast lanes, the endless shops selling endless plastic bottles for holy water, plastic everything. The commercialism and exploitation of people's faith was beyond belief! There were queues everywhere, for candles, for every kind of memento, at the slot machines to post prayers into. Mike reckoned the best queue of all was to buy a folding stool to sit on in the queue to get into Bernadette's holy grotto, as there would be at least a four hour wait. Needless to say, we didn't wait. We were off to Cathar country. We wanted to see how our own medieval castle compared with the real thing!

Montségur and Puivert castles were our first sights of these awesome stone strongholds, built atop high mountains as refuges for Cathar *parfaits* and their followers. The Christian sect, critical of the corruption in the established church, broke away from the Catholic faith during the twelfth century, believing in two principles/gods – Evil (the material) on earth and Good (the spiritual) in heaven, and in successive reincarnations. The Cathars (from the Greek *katharos*, meaning pure) believed they had to renounce the world and be non-violent, vegetarian and sexually abstinent. Dissent flourished in independent Languedoc. In 1209, Pope Innocent (!) III called for a mobilisation of the clergy in a crusade against these heretics, and Catholic troops under Simon de Montfort laid siege to many of the fortresses.

Often designed as solar calendars, the castles focussed light to enter at the times of the summer and winter solstices, for example, and shine on sacred locations inside. Montségur is an excellent example. Puivert had a more cultural association; poets and musicians would gather there. The elite of *Les Troubadours du Pays d'Oc* met there to play in 1170. The lamp bases in the Musicians' Hall are decorated with eight wonderful stone carvings of players of tabor drums, viols, lutes, *guiternes,* portable organs and other medieval musical instruments. These places just ooze history. Any site, such as Montségur, that has witnessed more than two hundred men and women being burnt at the stake is bound to have a chilling 'atmosphere', if you're open to it. Later in 1209, the crusade arrived at Béziers. Arnaud-Amaury, its spiritual leader, is said to have exclaimed "Kill them all! God will recognise his own". 20,000 citizens were massacred. Is the issue of religion any more enlightened some eight hundred years later?

Prades was next on our list of sights to see. Peg and Alan went there in 1962, and she writes briefly about the area and the Canigou, "a very noble mountain", in *Lilac and Roses*. We wanted to retread their steps and go and have a look ourselves. It is a magnificent mountain with the town of Prades nestling at its foot. We thought we'd treat ourselves to a hotel bed and found a reasonably priced one in the centre. As it happened, we had the least sleep of the whole trip. The hotel was on a high street and traffic, which you normally expect to taper off around midnight, didn't. We did have a pleasant meal there, however, and afterwards went for a stroll downtown. We were drawn to an alternative-looking café, from which issued, rather loudly, the dulcet tones of Van Morrison.

"How about a night cap and a bit of Van the Man, then?" As good an end to another Perfect Day as any!

Next day, we rather overdid it – not another Cathar stronghold! – as we visited Peyrepertuse and Quéribus. The weather wasn't entirely with us. Peyrepertuse, a long, narrow stone citadel hacked out of the craggy peak, is one of the most remote and difficult to get to. At 609m (2,000 ft), it was blowing a gale, and we didn't dare climb the perilous-looking steps to the highest part, especially with the sheer drop at the side. As the leaflet said, complete with typographical errors: "Safety instructions: The visit is dangerous in hight winds and stictly forbidden during storms. Stong shoes should be worn"! We took their word for it and made our way rather more safely down the mountain path through the woods to the bottom.

A MAN'S HOME IS HIS CASTLE (2000)

We had one day left. Just west of Narbonne lies Fontfroide Abbey, now Cistercian, once the bastion of the Catholic faith against the Cathar heresy. Monks from this abbey had to leave their solitude and return to the real world to fight in the crusade. It's a beautiful building inside from photographs, but we missed the start of a two-hour tour by a few minutes. It was a warm, sunny day, so we contented ourselves with a walk around the impressive exterior and up into the Perfumed Garden, full of honeysuckle, thyme, rosemary, citronella and old English roses. Sensational smells, but heavy competition was coming from the grand-looking kitchens where lunch was in preparation. Pretty soon, smart people began to show up in even smarter Shiny Toys. We pondered whether to stay and to hell with the expense, but it was *complet*. It obviously has a great reputation. We headed off into Narbonne for something more modest.

It was market day but not too busy now it was after noon. Mike and I are both fans (as long as it isn't busy) and love to browse and purchase the odd item we might need or fancy. We strolled along the riverbank, drinking in the different sights. Towns are a great stimulus when you've been out in the sticks. We had a two-hour 'fix', then drove on to the motorway and home. Two tasks awaited us before a visit from Ian and Tina in a week's time. We wanted to get back on our roof, while the good weather lasted, and have another go at stopping the infuriating leak. Water was obviously getting in through the neighbour's wall above, rather than through the fillet, which we'd checked so many times. We were determined to fill every crack and joint we could find. This required yet another circus balancing act, involving ladders and planks again, this time over the ridge of the roof. You'd think we'd be fed up with pointing stones by now, wouldn't you? We were, but we did it anyway.

We also fitted a new front door (glazed for extra light) and frame. Not easy, as no space is ever the regular shape it should be, and all jobs require a lot of 'fine tuning' to put it mildly. Ian and Tina came down by train this time, then bus from Valence to Aubenas, where we picked them up. It was a short and happy visit. We ate and drank well, walked it off and canoed on the

99

Ardèche, from Balazuc to Ruoms – only 7kms, but a thrilling first for all of us.

Mike and I had talked about extending our letting season to include Christmas and Easter, and we were going to install electrical heating in the *gîte*. Stoves and appliances are always *en promo* here in the autumn, and we bought well – eight wall-mounted heaters for a good price at Bricomarché in Aubenas. Mike had also renovated an old two-bar fire with glowing 'embers' that had belonged to my parents. We didn't like it too much, but on chilly nights we thought it might provide some psychological warmth. In the absence of a wood stove (no chimney in the lounge), this fire would have to do. I think wood fires are a must in winter in the country. We'd wait and see what the demand for winter holidays would be.

Out came the electrical toolbox and the reels of cable. We created a separate circuit linking all the fires to a pay meter. We were pretty sure that our current electrical power supply of 6Kw would not stand the strain, and when we put them all on at once, it blew. A visit was made to EdF (*Electricité de France*) to arrange an appointment for them to upgrade the supply (to 12Kw) and the meter (a new electronic one was required). But they were busy installing heaters. Their publicity about electric heating not being as expensive as most people thought, compared with wood and *fioul* (diesel) stoves, had obviously worked. We would have to wait until the beginning of December, they told us. Oh dear!

There was an awful lot of rain in November. The rivers Beaume and Drobie changed out of all recognition, and water once more poured out of the mountainsides. Water, water everywhere – in Canterbury too, apparently. The river Stour next to our house was also flooding.

- 7 -
FAME AND FORTUNE (2001)

WE SURVIVED the floods, though the water came very close to the house. The road was closed, and piles of sandbags were issued by the Council for use on doorways and gates. They didn't last long in a city full of students, who, well the worse for wear after the pubs close, thought it a 'good game' to throw all the bags in the river. (And these are the bright ones!) Such is contemporary life in Britain, and one of the reasons we're always so pleased to leave the country. We planned to go in style this year in a new van! The faithful Bedford had had its day. It was stripped – Mike discovered things in it he'd forgotten he had – and taken to the dump to be crushed. We searched around for a good deal and found a V-reg Peugeot Expert, that had been in a minor accident and was going for a good price – £6,000. It was very comfortable and we both felt happy driving it.

Even more exciting than a new van was the news that Léonie Press had agreed to publish my mum's book, *Lilac and Roses*! I'd 'published' (photocopied) an edited, home-made version of it for people staying in the *gîte* to read, if they were interested in the history of the house. After buying and reading one of the Léonie Press books, *Où est le 'ping'?*, I'd rung them and asked if I could send a copy of L&R to see if they thought it suitable. I was thrilled to bits when they came back to me with a swift and positive reply. One thing I learned is that every book that's published in Britain automatically goes into The British Library and the libraries of six universities – Oxford and Cambridge, London, Edinburgh, Cardiff and Belfast. This gives me a real thrill on Peg's behalf. Ian and I both agree that this would really have tickled her!

It was a pleasure getting to know Jack and Anne Loader, the publishers, and we worked together on the publicity for *Lilac and*

Roses. The book was launched at the France Shop in Canterbury, which sells everything the francophile could want, on 31 March 2001. We'd sent out releases to the local media, and the press had responded and were coming to take photos. Mike and I took in some bottles of Ardèche wine; Ian and Tina came down for the day to celebrate with us. We sold four copies, mainly to friends! But we had nice pieces in the Canterbury Times and the Kentish Gazette (tomorrow the world!), and I had a date with Radio Kent in a week's time. I wasn't a total novice with the media, having worked in PR and made quite a few radio and TV appearances already, so the short interview on Radio Kent was good fun rather than a nerve-racking experience. While we were at the studio, Mike and I also met Dave Cash, former DJ with Kenny Everett on pirate Radio Caroline (who remembers them from the sixties?), now a broadcaster on the station. That was another pleasure; I'd been a regular listener in my teens. The coincidence, too, is that Dave's son, Simon, works for those friends of ours who have an army surplus shop in Canterbury! Small world.

After the launch, we were free again to go to France. Usual life-change routine and, with a well-loaded van, inside and on the roofrack, we set off for the sun. Not to nearby Dover this time though. Even though we're only twenty-five minutes from the quickest (and most expensive) route across the channel to Calais, we'd become so sick of P&O and its fares policy (rip-off), that we'd decided to stop going this way. Their prices appear to be academic; you're given a different quotation each time you ring, depending on whom you talk to. I also have shares with them passed on from my parents, which should entitle us to a fifty per cent discount. But, guess what? The concessionary scheme does-n't apply to vans. Everyone who drives a van is a bootlegger, especially when it's loaded going from Britain to the continent, of course! And it isn't even a van – the Peugeot Expert Combi is actually a MPV, with windows and removable seats at the rear, but it's not on P&O's list of vehicles, so it doesn't exist. Anyway, we were tired of battling with them, so we voted with our feet, or rather our wheels, transferred our loyalty to Brittany Ferries, and were going Portsmouth-Le Havre overnight.

FAME AND FORTUNE (2001)

Remember how Maggie told us that consumerism would bring us all more choice and power? Choice maybe, too much of it. Confusion marketing. Quantity, not quality. But power? I don't think so. The goal posts move all the time. We both resent the majority being penalised because of the bad behaviour at least, crimes at worst, of the minority. This is only because powers-that-be won't address the minority; it's easier (and more cost-effective probably) to write them off as a bad debt. I'm certainly not for a police state, but the whole world's being run by accountants. Help! And, now (in 2003) the French are crying out for another Madame Thatcher of their own! It's all going to happen in France too.

En route to Portsmouth, we'd arranged to meet Louise and Lawrence, and Clare for a farewell meal in Hungerford, which was convenient for us all to get to, and for us to continue on to the port. We were impressed with the ferry; it was more like a cruise ship, not that either of us has ever been on one, but there were cinemas, a casino, a swimming pool, and we felt we were treated more like people than animals. We'd booked a cabin, but before we turned in, we went to the movies to see 'Bridget Jones' Diary', which we'd missed over the winter. It wasn't that good an idea actually, not because of the movie which we enjoyed, both having a soft spot for Hugh Grant, but it didn't finish until 11.30pm which meant we didn't have much time to sleep. They wake you at five am and you're off the ferry at seven. It was the year of the Foot and Mouth horror in Britain, and we'd been rather wary about going abroad. We'd phoned French friends in the Ardèche to get their reaction and they'd laughed at our concern. The French had dealt with their small outbreak rather differently and 'stopped' it (officially) within a short space of time. Nevertheless, in Le Havre, we had to drive the van, and walk, through disinfectant. But it didn't hold us up for long. We had a good journey and arrived in Ribes late afternoon.

Normally when we get here early April, our virginia creeper covering the terrace is just sprouting. We cut it back to the old wood each November, as its growth is so prolific. We didn't want there to be too much green yet, as Pergolas R Us were back in

103

business. We were going to build a covered and tiled pergola over our terrace to replace the *tonnelle* (metal pole supports) that was already there. This would give us a dry seating area outside, where we could eat and cater if it was raining, and offer us more protection from the sun in high summer – another room outside, in effect. The creeper was years old and we didn't want to lose it. There's also a precious red climbing rose and a beautiful honey-suckle growing there too. The foliage's cool green provides a thick screen between us and guests, giving some privacy if they use the other part of the terrace. So the problem was how to support all this plant life, whilst dismantling the poles and building a wooden pergola in their place. It needed a fiendish plan.

I can't even remember how we did it. All I know is that it was down to Mike and we succeeded. He also managed to extract the pole structure, shorter but intact, to be reused to make an *abri* (shelter) over by the veggie patch, where I could keep tools and pot up plants. *"Il n'est pas bête"* (he's not stupid), the neighbours said, as they watched the new wooden construction take shape.

"Ce ne sera pas comme chez vous," (It won't look like yours) I told the Balazucs. *"On ne met pas de tuiles, mais des 'shingles'."* (We're putting shingles on, not tiles.) I held up a sample, not knowing whether this new bit of *franglais* we'd picked up at the builders' yard had yet filtered through to him. Christian looked a bit concerned, as it's not the done way here.

"Ce ne sera visible que de chez nous, pas de chez vous." (It'll only be visible from our place.) He didn't look convinced, but when it was finished, we received many compliments, both from him and others. *"C'est un artiste, ton mec,"* they said. Another winner.

Spring is a beautiful season everywhere; it's one of the best for us, along with autumn, in the Ardèche. The weather was hot, as it often is in May. Our garden was looking just lovely, bursting with life and colour, parasols and hammocks up, furniture out and oiled with linseed, paths and steps neat and weed-free, tomato and salad plants growing well in the veg patch, geraniums, begonias and petunias potted up – *nickel* (the business)! Our first guests arrived late in the month, on a motorbike, but all was not well. John had a large bandage round his ankle. They'd had a mishap, stopped to park the bike, and it had fallen on his foot. He was in quite a lot of pain, but after hospital treatment he'd decided he'd be able to make it down here, even a day late, so they could have their holiday after all.

The next day we had a hailstorm we'll never forget. We were all sitting on the terrace when it suddenly arrived. The stones were the size of golf balls! A cry of shock was heard from Roberte over the road, as she emerged from her housework inside. She virtually threw herself on to her new terrace dining table, to stop its glass top from breaking! Mike rushed over to help her move it to shelter and on his way back got hit by a hailstone on the head, which nearly knocked him out! The noise on our new terrace roof was like machine-gun fire. The courtyard was white in seconds and covered, too, with a mass of broken-off branches and twigs, plants and flowerheads all over the ground. The hail lasted five minutes and caused complete devastation. We watched in despair as shrubs and plants were flattened, but I nevertheless had to get my camera. We needed a photo – no-one would believe it. When it was over, Joyce collected a large bag of hailstones to pack round John's ankle. Waste not, want not!

Nature is a force to be reckoned with; it should have far, far more respect paid it. A week or so later, with all the debris cleared up, everything just started sprouting again. Within a month, you wouldn't have known it had happened. Our tomato plants had been ruined and had to be replaced – there was naturally a sudden rush on them and new ones were hard to find. Others who'd suffered from this narrow band of extreme weather were in the same boat. The vines at Lablachère had been particularly badly hit, and a gloomy wine year was predicted in the *cave coopérative*. A similar storm had happened in July eighteen years ago. I remembered Peg and Alan telling me about it. The hailstone drifts had lasted two days, despite the high temperatures, rooftiles had been smashed and car roofs dented like colanders. We'd come off lightly this time.

The summer seemed to fly by. We lived an awful lot outside, making the most of our new 'room'. We had guests returning to La Clède, cementing the friendships made before, our annual picnic with *les Belges,* lots of other partying – the French are great *fêtards* (party goers) – often into the early hours or all night. It's a very sociable time, as families come together and tourists pour into the area. There are markets, day and night, outdoor events, concerts of music of all kinds, theatre, village *fêtes* and lots of entertainment for the kids. Then, suddenly, at the end of August, it's all over and everyone's talking about *la rentrée* (going back to school), which is the next big event in the French calendar. Shops which have been open all day in the season suddenly go back to closing from midday to three pm. It always takes us by surprise. At first, it seems a nuisance, but we actually prefer these sleepier ways. Shopkeepers and market traders have time to talk again, and you feel you have the place back to yourselves.

We had more returnees in early September – our 'Czech mates'[*] – back to canoe the Ardèche again, as they're great enthusiasts. Louise and Lawrence were here at the same time, and all eight of us planned to go canoeing together – the full Monty – the whole 32 kilometres, from before Pont d'Arc to St Martin. It was a wonderful experience. Seeing the gorges from river level is even better than from above. We had to stop a great deal to bail out the canoes, but we didn't fall out or really disgrace ourselves. (The photographers wait at certain difficult rapids to catch all gaffes on film, and caught us doing one backwards!) We were pretty tired by the end, and the home straight seemed to go on forever. But we were definitely high on the trip and opened the champagne as soon as we got back to Ribes. Milan excused himself, took his glass inside to listen to the World Service news, and came out looking white as a sheet. It was September 11. New York's twin towers had been blasted off the skyline. The news shook the world. It took us all a long time to recover.[**]

The Czechs had stayed with our friends, Jeff and Renée the previous year, as we were already booked up. They'd all become

---

[*] They left Prague for England in 1968, a few days before the Russian tanks rolled in.

[**] Joni reacted to these events by doing a series of four paintings - her first of social commentary - which can be seen on her latest (last?) album, *Travelogue* (Reprise, 2002).

good friends too and had had a short holiday in Prague together. (Little did we know that we would be seeing their beautiful capital ourselves in the near future.) They bought Mike and me a Czech cookbook, knowing how much we enjoy cooking, and we'd promised to prepare a meal for all of us. There were nine of us at the lunch on our terrace under our pergola: Peter and Virginia, Milan and Bella, Jeff and Renée, Gunhi, Louise and Lawrence, Mike and I. Louise, a vegetarian, and Lawrence helped us out with the cooking; they made the *bramborák* (potato pancakes); I made the garlic soup and a vegetarian goulash; Mike made the beef goulash. He cooked it all day and the meat just fell apart. They said it was the best goulash they'd ever tasted, and we know they weren't just being polite; they're not like that!

When everyone had left and we'd all cleared up, Lawrence and Mike stood outside looking up at the millions of stars, and Lawrence apparently said:

"Don't you ever feel guilty, Mike?"

"What about?"

"Well, we've got to go home and back to work. You'll just stay and carry on enjoying all this!"

And so we do! And, now it was October; we were free again and about to have a holiday as well! Time for more "picture postcard charms"*.

Now Mike was and is a cycling fanatic. In his late teens, he was racing – long and short distance – and winning – regularly. But plans for a future in cycling were halted by polio at age nineteen. Because of his strength and fitness, he recovered well and was able to resume, but never attained the same speeds and levels of endurance. In his early twenties, though, he was commuting to work and back by bike, twenty-seven miles each way! His interest in the sport has never palled. So, this holiday, one of the places we were going was Mont Ventoux, one of the hardest *cols* on the *Tour de France*. I'll hand over to him for this one:

"From the Ardèche mountains, it's not a long trip across the Rhône to Mont Ventoux, which had been well up on my list of

---

* From Amelia, *Hejira* album

'Journeys To Make' for some time. Tom Simpson, arguably England's most famous racing cyclist, Olympic medallist, world champion and the first Briton to wear the coveted Tour leader's yellow jersey, collapsed and died racing up Ventoux in *canicule* heat on 13 July 1967. Simpson was incredibly popular, a hero in France as well as Britain. On 14 July, his British team-mate, Barry Hoben, broke away from the *peloton* (the middle field), and the riders there refused to chase him down, as an indication of their feelings, allowing him to win the next stage. This was an incredible thing to happen and to my knowledge hasn't occurred before or since. I wanted to visit Simpson's memorial, built on the spot he died, just two kilometres from the summit. It was a very strange and emotional moment for me, as we stood there, reading the words on the marble slab, looking at all the old bike parts traditionally left by fans and other cyclists – we'd brought a pedal – who like me had come to pay homage to "Major Tom" (as the French press christened him). The mountain is such an eerie, barren place; nothing grows in the almost white shale – from a distance, it appears to be snow-capped – and it's like Walking On The Moon. Jan seemed as moved as I at the atmosphere of the place. She hugged me then wandered off, leaving us both to our thoughts, before we drove – shamefully, we felt, past more aspiring, and perspiring, cyclists – to the summit. It was a special day for me and I even bought the guide book as a souvenir!"

I'll just briefly mention one delightful stop we made on the way to Ventoux which was at Suze la Rousse. In this modest village we discovered a mighty *château* which now houses the *Université du Vin*. The French take these things seriously – quite rightly! – especially now they've competition from the New World. Inside there was a terrific exhibition of naive paintings entitled *Art Brut – Vigne et Vin,* and examples of old wine-making equipment, and we passed a very happy two hours or so. After Ventoux, we went south-east to retread Peg and Alan's steps once again and explore the Gorges du Verdon. First stop: Moustiers Sainte Marie, which was horribly touristy and commercialised, especially its overly decorated and overly priced pottery. We camped in a beautiful site in the valley, looking up at the two mountain peaks with the famous star strung across between them. According to provençal writer Mistral, a knight taken prisoner in the Holy Land during the seventh crusade in 1249 made this vow: "At your feet, Virgin Mary, I will hang my chain, if ever I return to Moustiers, my homeland."

Aiguines has another attractive (17th century) *château*, flanked by four pepperpot turrets with coloured glazed tiles, and was home of the last of the witches of Provence, Mother Bousquet, familiar with all the plants growing on the Verdon cliffs and fabricator of a multitude of healing potions and liquors – brambles for angina, lavender for insect and snake bites and so on. "No disease could resist her, and people came from afar to consult the old 'mask.'" Herbs are another of my passions.

The first sight of the emerald water* of the Lac de Sainte Croix takes your breath away, and you barely get it back throughout the whole of the circuit of the Verdon canyon, the deepest in Europe. The landscape is just magnificent – almost too vast and wild to take in, and the only other region in France that has impressed me more than the Ardèche. Even in October, there are always trippers at sights like this and, as you all 'do the gorges', stopping to gaze in awe at all the same places, you get quite chummy with each other. We talked to some Americans, who, while naturally comparing it with the Grand Canyon, said they preferred Verdon, as it was "so much more manageable. The Grand Canyon is just too big!" (Read in Chapter 9 about our brief visit there.)

At another viewing point, we were all amazed and enchanted to see a young boar emerging from the scrubland at the side of the road right up close to us. It wasn't wild, as it was obviously used to humans, but it was very ragged-looking and starving hungry. I threw some bread to it from about two feet away and it shot its snout up towards me and nearly had my hand off. All baby animals are cute but boar are not to be played with. They can be very nasty indeed. (Christian has told us many scary hunting tales of encounters with them. We even got to see one that his team had shot. It was a real biggie with huge tusks and weighed in at well

---

* The water in the Verdon, meaning gift of green, gets its deep green colour from the fluorine it contains acting on minute algae therein.

over one hundred kilos.)

We stopped for a coffee at the Hotel du Grand Canyon, perched on the side of La Falaise des Cavaliers. From the terrace outside, cantilevered over the canyon, there's a sheer drop of more than 400 metres to the bottom. Absolutely don't lean over if you suffer from vertigo! We thought it a fantastic spot – no other signs of civilisation whatsoever – a great place to stay for a few days of hiking or just being away from it all. At various other sheer drop locations, climbers gathered to scale the cliffs. We couldn't get over how they'd fix their rope hooks to rings in the rocks and then just leap over the side in the most death-defying way to drop at an alarming speed to the bottom, only to climb all the way up again! Everyone has their own way of getting their kicks, don't they?! We neither of us remotely fancy bunji-jumping either! (Mike's daughter, Clare, on the other hand has done every thrill going, from parachuting to sand surfing to gorge swinging! Don't ask! She said it was ten times worse than bunji-ing, so she did it twice!)

Onwards to Castellane with its Virgin statue and chapel, Notre Dame du Roc, built high on the mountain backdrop, the Lac de Castillon, formed by a hydroelectric dam in the Verdon river. Visits to Gordes (not nearly as nice as Cordes), the eerie stone Village des Bories, Sorgues, famous for its very deep source of the river Vaucluse, where we just wanted a drink and they wanted a fortune just to park, so we left! For our last night this trip, we found a lovely B&B in the charming village of St Didier, then made our way back home via Orange. This is a large and busy, but undaunting town, where we parked without hassle and spent several pleasant hours wandering around and taking in some of its Roman past at the Arc de Triomphe, the Arena and nearby museum.

Our beautiful neighbour, Roberte, Christian's wife, was fifty on 12 October and the family was having a bit of a do at the Salle Polyvalente (village hall). Dress to be very formal – khaki/camouflage/army surplus! This, of course, is the favourite attire of all the hunters and a fashion item for their 'molls'. It suited us both down to the ground too. Mike's worn it for years, thanks in great part to friends, Paul and Mel and their surplus stores, and I love it because it's comfy, well-made and durable, a good colour for me – and cheap! All the family was there, including the kids, of course, plus friends, making a total of around fifty. Vast quantities of food (we had to go back the next day for leftovers and Take Two!), wine, conviviality, chatter and loud music in a large, echo-y hall, brilliantly decorated with swathes of army camo netting, camo fabrics and black and green balloons. About four hours of this is enough for me. Mike, too, probably less, though he's happy to watch and smile – and dance. Only one thing wrong there. Orane had currently taken a shine to Rock Around The Clock by Bill Haley, so we had to listen to that at least six times! Not one of my faves. And, unfortunately, neither Mike nor I can jive – <u>properly</u>.

Oddly enough, three more of my female friends, all Scorpios, were also soon about to be fifty. Anne, whom we'd met in Canterbury, via France Shop, who was thinking, with Keith, her partner of moving to France to live and looking for some first-hand experiences. Apparently, most of the people they'd talked the idea through with were quite negative. We certainly weren't. Now, they're over here permanently and loving it; Glynis, a friend from way back when we were both North London landladies and SWELLS (Single Women Earning Lots and Lots, well, not lots, but enough!); and Rita, ex-neighbour in Canterbury, now in Devon. Rita had invited nine of her friends to spend three days celebrating with her in a hideaway cottage in Helford, Cornwall. We were going back, rather earlier than last year, to do just that. Prior to that, though, we had plans for our kitchen.

We needed a decent cooker and a bigger fridge (we already had a medium freezer). We went to Leader in Aubenas. (This is a chain like Comet in the UK.) They had a large selection of both and at good prices, some *en promo*, and very knowledgeable and helpful staff. We chose our models. The demonstration cooker was the only one in stock, but with a damaged lid/top, which they said they would replace and deliver to us with our chosen fridge freezer (too big for the van for once!) They pulled out the cooker, and there was a replacement lid already behind it. Were we on mains or bottled gas? They changed the lid, converted it for bottles there and then and helped us to load it. When the large fridge/freezer was delivered a few days later, a young man single-handedly pulled it across our gravelled courtyard on his trolley, up the steps, over the doorway step and into the kitchen, where he proceeded to unwrap it, check the inside and give us a short talk on its functions and benefits. Then, with a broad smile and a *Bonne journée*, he was gone.

(Compare this to a recent visit to Comet in Canterbury, again on the lookout for a fridge. Ignored for more than fifteen minutes, no fridges in stock, "No, you can't have the demonstration model." "I thought this was a shop, not a shop window." Then, queuing for at least ten minutes at the sales counter, while mini-mal staff were unhelpful and inefficient with other customers, told about a ten day wait and a hefty delivery charge. We tore up the slip and left, to find a man with a clipboard outside, doing customer research on Comet! We certainly let our frustration out, apologised for taking it out on him, but made him laugh! Much more entertaining than most of his questionnaire-ees, he said.)

So we had our new appliances. Now we could build some units around them. We'd acquired some free melamine (old dis-play units) – after asking first, of course – from the *poubelles* (waste bins) behind 'But', another chain store. From this, Mike built some dry food storage units and wine cupboards to go along one side of our fridge/freezers. On the other side, we kept a large shelving unit in pine that was already there. Kitchen half-finished, with food, drink and crockery storage all sorted. Next year we would tackle the other side, with units around sink and cooker.

At the end of a rather wet October, Joyeuse held its annual *Salon Gourmand*, when everyone celebrates the new *primeur* Gamay wine, and there is much munching of roast chestnuts to accompany this. It's usually a very jolly family affair with food stalls and street entertainment, but this year the drizzly weather took the edge off for us. Rain seems to dampen French spirits rather less, however, and as long as there's wine and food, they're happy! We're usually not at all happy leaving Ribes, but we were going to party in Cornwall.

Helford is lovely, quintessentially English, and apparently the setting for Daphne du Maurier's *Frenchman's Creek*. We had mild sunshine there and spent much time outside walking in the beautiful, autumnal countryside around the water's edge or sitting on the cottage's garden terrace, reading and chatting with the others, some of whom we already knew. A real luxury for us all, we were to be catered for, morning and evening, and we were presented with a full English breakfast if we wanted it. We all had the works the first day – it's something we never have in France – but by the third day were groaning and having "just one lightly poached egg and toast, thanks"! The evening meals were excellent – a chef came in to cook for us – and after a day's activity we were hungry and absolutely delighted with all the dishes he prepared. It was a brilliant idea and a really nice 'do', ending with a special birthday meal with prezzies and posh frocks and suits on the last evening.

A daytime highlight was a visit to The Eden Project[*] – The Living Theatre of Plants and People – in nearby St Austell. Groups of gigantic biomes (conservatories) now stand on the site of a former derelict clay quarry. These are "living laboratories, showing the plants we depend on as they grow in the wild together, and a living demonstration of how man has gradually domesticated and farmed them." These biomes create different climate zones – humid (rain forest), warm (Mediterranean) and semi-arid (desert), uncompleted when we were there, and are full to bursting with the appropriate flora – just amazing places to walk around and learn so much. From the Introduction of *Eden: the first book (2000)*:- "Eden isn't so much a destination as a place in the heart. It's not just a marvellous piece of science-related architecture, it is also a statement of our passionate belief in an optimistic future for mankind. Within this showcase, Eden will tap into some fundamental truths, and prompt some fundamental questions about our relationship with nature; about what we are doing right, what we are doing wrong, and what we are going to do about it.

"We may all have feet of clay but that shouldn't stop us trying

---

[*] Bodelva, St Austell, Cornwall PL242SG. Tel: 01726 811911, Fax: 01726 811912, www.edenproject.com

to make a difference. Wouldn't we all rather look back and say "I'm glad I did" rather than "I wish I had"?

The vision of the project's instigator, Tim Smit and his team, is brilliant and we're so full of admiration for them and their determination, despite so many odds. Eden is a symbol of regeneration. All this flora, growing on degraded land, shows that environmental improvement is possible. Now, he really is someone who's trying – and succeeding – in getting us "back to the garden".[*]

---

[*] From Woodstock, *Ladies of the Canyon* album

- 8 -
BACK TO THE GARDEN (2002)

MIKE WAS sixty-five in January, officially an OAP. His daughter, Louise came round to visit us the weekend before his birthday. Over coffee, she handed him an envelope containing his card, and he put it on one side with some other early ones.

"I think you'd better open it now," she said mysteriously. "There may be things you have to do." Very curious now, Mike tore open the envelope. Inside the card were two plane tickets to Prague and a hotel voucher. We stared at each other in amazement.

"It's from Lawrence and Clare too," she added. "That's incredible, Louise," we both said. "What a fabulous present! Thank you so much." The flight was in four days' time.

"Hope your passports are valid. *Bon voyage!*"

We loved Prague – an enchanted place. The "city of a hundred spires", which, unlike many other major European cities, has never been bombed, just invaded – many times, leaving (guide book speak) "an impossible, almost surreal treasure trove of Romanesque, Gothic, Baroque, Art Nouveau and Cubist architecture". The buildings are gracious and lovely, especially now the facades are changing from communist grey to pastels. The inhabitants have endured many hardships over the centuries. Today's young don't suffer in silence and there is much graffiti everywhere. Our hotel wasn't too far from Wenceslas Square[*] and the centre of the city.

We had three whole days to 'do' it. Absolutely impossible! It

---

[*] Nor the young of the previous generation. It was the anniversary of Jan Palach's death and there were many wreaths there. Jan Palach was a philosophy student who set himself alight to protest against the occupation in 1968 by the armies of the Warsaw Pact

was –5°C and snowing when we arrived. Guide book again: "In winter the views are even more magical; no city wears its mantle of snow more beautifully". So true. We walked until we dropped and when we dropped, we took the trams. What a brilliantly quick and efficient way to get around and look and look. The beautiful river Vltava with its bridges, the opera house, the cathedral, the castle, the palace, the old town, the Jewish town. For culture, the Mucha museum (so much exquisite Art Nouveau because of Mucha), Andy Warhol at the National Gallery, even a puppet show of the Beatles' Yellow Submarine. Shops burst with colourful Bohemian crystal glass. It's what tourists buy (and Bata shoes as well). Food and drink are good and cheap, if you leave the tourist routes and go to the pubs and restaurants frequented by the Czechs themselves. Much beer is consumed but with little destruction or violence afterwards, as far as we could see. Most people earn very little, we were told, but get stoically on with their lives. I always knew I'd empathise with the place; there's got to be something very different going on, if President Vaclav Havel can propose Frank Zappa[*] for Minister of Culture!

We left early for France this year with new money in our wallets (and a computer amongst many other things in the van). The euro was now in use, though all bills and bank statements had been in both currencies for a couple of years already, to get us all used to it. Our first guests were due to arrive in mid-April – an Australian couple was staying at La Clède for a month. They have a farm near Perth and produce their own wine, a bottle of which they brought with them for us to try, a Cabernet Sauvignon called Spring Hill. Very good it was too. We tried it out on Christian, who's very particular about his wines, thinking we might broaden his horizons somewhat!

"*C'est pas terrible. Je préfère les vins français!*" (It's OK. I prefer French wines), was his rather predictable, chauvinistic reaction! It made Tony laugh anyway; he's well aware of French views generally on New World wines. He and wife Trish, both francophiles, come to a different wine area every other year. More generous

---

[*] American rock guitarist, songwriter, with his band The Mothers of Invention

than our neighbour, he was extremely complimentary about those he tasted in the Ardèche, which incidently has won more prizes for its wine than any other French *département*, many from a place called Alba la Romaine, near Montélimar, though none has Appellation as yet[*].

We took them to meet Jeff and Renée, who also make their own – similarly, around 200-250 litres a year – and the exchange was an extremely pleasant one. Everyone's always impressed with J-F & R, who are both absolutely charming, knowlegeable and helpful, and the location of their house, set just below Beaumont and over-looking the wild Drobie valley. It's a beautifully peaceful place to live, yet only half an hour from civilisation. Tony gave us great tips on olive conservation and vine pruning with very successful results the following year. We got very friendly over the four weeks and there was Not A Dry Eye In The House when they left us. We're planning to go visit them in 2004.

First event in our French social calendar 2002 was Christian's 50th birthday party, which took place in brother Eric's and wife Carole's lovely new house, just completed further up the mountain. The usual *'grande bouffe'* (blow-out) at midday, still going strong at 5pm, their two young kids, Charlotte and Matthias both insisting they dance with everyone. Mike made him a birthday cake, one of our favourites from Linda McCartney's *On Tour*[**], Naughty Nougat Cake. He put toasted almonds all around the edge. *"Il y en a combien?"* asked Christian. *"Cinquante? Tu l'as fait exprès?"* (How many are there? Fifty? Deliberately?)

"Non," replied Mike, which was the truth. Christian counted them. There were indeed fifty, which was an amazing and delightful coincidence!

Mike was equally delighted a few weeks later, when he got the van reregistered and his new 07 number. We left the *sous-préfecture* in Largentière, clutching our precious *carte grise,* and got the plates made up there and then by a guy with a mobile unit parked opposite. Great enterprise, great service – such things are much

---

[*] Côtes du Vivarais wines now have AOC (Appellation d'Origine Controllé).
[**] *On Tour* by Linda McCartney (Time Warner, 1998)

appreciated by us. We also came to appreciate the different treatment we received, driving a van with local plates, notably in late season when the Ardechois who are still working run out of patience with tourists taking their time because they're on holiday or just lost. An 07 van has a bit of clout! People give way to us – they don't behave quite the same when we're in my insignificant Renault 5! But, in both vehicles, we always have a laugh when other drivers spot the 07, then look in amazement and shock that the driver's not where they expect, on the left, but on the right!

We were going to have a lot of visits from friends and family this year, and there's nothing like visitors to goad you into action on the home improvement front! We had our kitchen to finish. The actual layout didn't change, as the existing plan worked well; it was simply a question of building units and fitting doors (thank you again, Derek). One huge improvement, though, was a new (but old-fashioned looking) ceramic sink, to replace the old butler, but at the right height, which was going to save our backs! Years ago, Serge had put the butler sink in – too low. I'd joked with him that he still thought of me as a kid, but I'd grown since! Anyway, the new one was just bliss, and the end result looked really swish with everything in white, including white tiled worktops. With red accessories. Mike had started collecting kitchen stuff in red in 1996 when he was living a lonely life above the shop in Canterbury. We also had a set of red pans and matching wok already here. And that was how it started. Every time we went to a *brocante* or a charity shop, we seemed to find another item to add, a jug or a colander. We were aided and abetted by Mike's sister, Betty, who's an incurable jumble sale addict. We've stopped the addiction now – everything in moderation! – but it's a good choice and contrasts well with the cool grey stone walls in the room, so that it's warming in the cold and bright in the light and heat.

Roberte liked it, though she always says nice things about the work we do both in the house and garden. *"Quelle belle cuisine intégrée,"* she said enviously, looking around. (What a lovely fitted kitchen.) *"J'en voudrais une, mais je crois que Christian ne la fera jamais."* (I'd like one too, but I don't think Christian will ever do it.)

She tutted to herself and sighed. But she makes some pretty fine *cuisine* in that – albeit dated – kitchen of hers, as we know all too well. The best pastry in the Ardèche, for starters!

Both Mike and I love to cook too, but in very different ways. Mike spent a short time as a trainee cook at Lyons Corner House just off Piccadilly Circus in the fifties – remember those? – and he'd had his own highly successful café for five years in Whitstable. He's therefore extremely professional and can cut an onion in seconds flat, just like those chefs on the television! And he prefers to work to recipes. I, on the other hand, like to make dishes up and experiment and really only enjoy cooking for people I like. (The most fun for me is knocking up a meal spontaneously with what's in the fridge and the cupboard, as we keep a good stock of basics.) So I'm OK cooking for us, or friends and family, but would be a disaster in a restaurant! We make a good team, providing one of us plays the role of *sous chef* when the other's doing their thing!

The soil here is generally very fertile. In a book about the parish/commune of Ribes, written in 1944, our part of it is described thus: *"La region qui s'étale en pente douce du Gelly à la rivière est un vrai jardin. Elle est abondamment plantée en vignes, mûriers, oliviers, châtagniers et arbres fruitiers divers."* (The area, which slopes gently down from the Gelly, the hamlet above ours, to the river, is a real garden. It's heavily planted with vines, mulberry, olive, chestnut and other fruit trees.)

Mike always says I'm the gardener, but he's getting more and more interested and has become a lily enthusiast, since I mentioned they're one of my favourite flowers. He's even joined the Royal Horticultural Society's Lily Group and has planted over thirty around the garden, mainly in the courtyard, and some beautiful, large and fragrant ones called Everest in Peg's Bed. We've over eighty shrubs and fifty trees in the garden, some of which are fruit trees, and we've had much enjoyment over the years finding different uses for the produce. For example:-

Cherries: we bottle in brandy syrup; make jam; or freeze for cooking (eg, *clafoutis* and tarts) and to eat, defrosted, in muesli

Mulberries: freeze for cakes and icecream – it's an incredible violet colour

Peaches: we love them grilled with a little sugar and *crême de pêche.*

Apricots: no more – we did have two apricot trees but they died, this year and last – they will only have a limited life here, apparently.

Greengages: fresh or jam.

Mirabelle plums: lovely sharp jam and flans.

Figs: brilliant chutney

Pears: cook whole in red wine and bottle; stew with chestnut honey; also make good chutney.

Pomegranates[*]: peel and freeze the small red fruits; they add great colour to fruit salads and tarts. We also give one each to family and friends every year (for good fortune, apparently). They dry well and can be sprayed silver and gold to make tasteful Chrissie deckers!

Rhubarb: two/three good crops a year, from which we make a purée; delicicous with *fromage frais* and freezes well.

Redcurrants: our neighbour Anne Gaudemar, gives us a *plateau* every year, a tradition which she started with my mum. We freeze some and make a fantastic, tart *sorbet* with the rest.

Grapes: we only have six old vines currently; we eat fresh (also freeze well like cherries) and make juice[**].

Hazelnuts: eaten fresh.

Chestnuts: roasted and bottled – neither of us likes *marrons glacés* much, preferring them savoury.

Walnuts: eaten fresh, though this year we've tried pickling some.

Olives: on Tony (from Perth)'s advice, we put these in a heavy saline solution for six months, transferred them to plain water for

---

[*] Peg used to tell me how hungry she'd been at college during the war and how she'd take hours to eat one with a pin to lessen her pangs. She planted the tree, which has lovely, vivid orange flowers in June/July.

[**] Grapes are a uniquely nourishing, strengthening, cleansing and regenerative food - Mahatma Ghandi drank grape juice during his marathon fasts. We plan to plant six Muscat grapevines next spring to replace the dead apricot trees.

several days, changing this every day to remove much of the saltiness, and then bottled them in oil with garlic and herbs.

As well as all this – all free – we have continuous salads, rocket, perpetual spinach, onions and leeks, tomatoes, cucumbers and usually some beans too, plus a generous herb garden. It's hardly self-sufficiency, but we wouldn't starve! We let Georges Delubac further down the village grow the veggies. A few years ago he had a well sunk. He only had to go down about 150m and now has an endless supply of free water. From him we can get all we need, all organic – carrots, beetroot, courgettes, aubergines, leeks, potatoes, beans, tomatoes and salads if we should run out, and the best eggs in the world – eat those once and you're spoiled for life!

Georgeanne Brennan, author of *In the French Kitchen Garden – the joys of cultivating a potager*[*], says "I'm a passionate believer in *potagers* and their worth, both in the kitchen and to the spirit." The introduction to her book reads: "In France, the kitchen garden, or *potager*, has for centuries been a cornerstone of the country way of life. Much more than a vegetable patch, the French kitchen garden is a communion between the indoors and the outdoors – a means of living in harmony with the earth, culminating in simple, elegant meals prepared fresh with the flavours of the season. Growing a *potager* is a life-affirming, enriching pursuit that can be easily adapted to almost any climate or lifestyle." I'll drink to that!

The French go mad for free food, wild mushrooms being one of the best examples. *Cèpes* and *girolles* are particularly highly prized, and in the right conditions, if you know where to look, you can find quite a lot in the woods around here. Most of the locals keep their special places a secret, of course! We usually get a few field mushrooms in the garden too. One of our favourite plants is *pourpier* (purslane), a ground-covering succulent. Its cultivated, flowering form is a wonderful container plant, needing barely any soil or water, and producing lovely multicoloured blooms from the same plant throughout the summer months. The wild version, a weed – you'll know straight away if you have it because you can't get rid of it! – is edible and apparently very

---

* Published 1998, Chronicle Books, California, USA

121

good for the heart. Eat the leaves raw in a mixed salad, or cooked, it makes a delicious tart.

Half-bake a pastry case in a tart dish. Meanwhile, fry in olive oil: garlic, *lardons* (small pieces of bacon), onion, and a mix of *pourpier* plus any of the following – spinach, *blettes* or nettle leaves, plus a few of sorrel. Spread this mixture in the pastry case, top with grated cheese (*gruyère* or *Emmental)* and bake until brown. Add eggs and milk/cream to the mixture to make a *quiche* version. Use nettle tips for this and put the rest of the plants in a dustbin of water and let them rot down. It smells pretty foul but you won't get a better fertiliser to water your container plants than this.

We had another drains crisis in June – one of the original concrete drainpipes from the *gîte* was blocked (and we thought we'd finished with all that!) Most thankfully, we had some tolerant and sympathetic guests at the time! It had to be roots growing through cracks again, and it meant digging up the flowerbed below our terrace to investigate. This would involve the removal of an enormous *deutzia* shrub in the centre, but more seriously, the death of the topiary reclining cat that I'd cut a few years back. This had been quite a talking point for neighbours and visitors – and a stopping point of interest on ramblers' walks around the village! Above it, the virginia creeper growing over the pergola, with its porthole 'windows' for eyes, looked like the head of an owl – The Owl and the Pussycat, which had graced and surveyed the courtyard. But the cat had to go – it was now too big and in the way. I just hadn't the heart to get rid of it all at once. The body came off first, leaving the head like the Cheshire Cat in *Alice in Wonderland*! We worked around it, having first tried to ascertain exactly where to dig. We had some idea of the pipe layout from previous excavations, but we didn't want to dig for nothing, especially not in the concrete ramp!

The obvious person to ask was Serge, who'd been involved in the building works for my parents with brother Geo, Christian's dad. We rang and asked him to come over – a site visit would be the only way to jog his memory. The drains, after all, had been laid some thirty-five years or more ago. He came, he looked, he reflected; then, with his right foot, he drew an arc where he thought the pipe entered the *puits perdu* (soakaway). If we got that right, we had a digging line backwards to locate the pipe. D'you know, he was spot on! We dug, we found it. I rang him that evening.

"*Serge, tu es un génie, tu sais! Quelle mémoire tu as! On l'a trouvé le tuyau!*" (You're a genius. What a memory! We've found the pipe!) "*Tiens, 'ben, tant mieux!*" (I could almost feel his glow of pleasure over the line!) "*Y a plus de trente-cinq ans qu'on l'a installé! Mais, bon courage avec le chantier!*" (Good, then, and good luck with the work!)

Once we'd removed the old pipe, replaced it with a plastic one and filled in the hole, we found ourselves with a large area of bare soil in the entrance flowerbed – not the best first impression for future guests. Again thankfully, we had friendly returnees staying next, but we needed to do a quick makeover. Oh no, not another visit to the *pépinière* (nursery)! I can't be trusted to control my plant addiction there, even though there are now few spaces left in the garden! We wanted to do blue and yellow in this bed. So, we went to the nursery and we bought:-

- 2 *ceanothus horizontalis* (blue flowers in spring and again in autumn, weather permitting)
- 1 *genêt* (gorse – vivid yellow mass of flowers in spring)
- 2 *festucca glauca* (blue grasses) – all she had (we found five more by the river – it grows wild here, but it's not such a vivid blue)
- 3 blue *agapantha*
- 5 *eryngium* (blue thistles)
- 1 *if* (yew) tree
- 1 *cyprès* (cypress) tree.

These latter were to be our own personal trees, Mike the yew, me the cypress[*]. We transplanted the *deutzia* higher up the garden. It was so big we had to hack it into two pieces with an axe! It was touch and go at one point, because of the timing and the heat,

---

[*] If we still have La Clède, when the time comes, we'd like our ashes put there. Families, please note.

but they both survived to bloom again.

And then our visitors began to arrive. First, in July, came Ron and Gerry on their way to a *gîte* in Italy (Ron's learning Italian), followed by Lauren in early August. On the evening of her arrival we went out to eat at one of our favourite local places. L'Auberge des Deux Aygues (*aygue* is the occitan word for water/river, *agua* in Spanish) lies at the junction of the two rivers Beaume and Drobie, about fifteen minutes drive away. It's very informal and we eat outside overlooking the rivers. They make the best pizzas ever and in July and August have musical *animations/soirées*, either live or on video. Tonight was salsa night with a live band. Mark and Mieke, two Belgian friends from Ribes came with us. Lauren, who can talk the hind legs off the proverbial donkey (affection-ately called The Mouth by us) was nicknamed Laurens of Australia by Mark, who likes to make jokes! She actually spent a lot of time dancing with the kids who are always around in French restaurants, and usually incredibly well behaved, I have to say. We joined them in a bop or two, when the band had warmed up. It was a great evening and a good start to an unusual week to come.

The saga of Mike's relationship with Lauren (and her brother Stefan) is a complicated one and could fill a book in itself. As it was, Lauren had just recently appeared on John Peel's Radio 4 programme *Home Truths*, telling the world a small part of it. Mike lost contact with them both when they were very young – Lauren, 4 and Stefan, 3 – but refound Lauren years later, through an amaz-ing coincidence, when she was going out with Paul, Mike's army surplus friend. It was Paul's mother, Barbara, who made the con-nection through separate conversations with Mike and with Lauren about their pasts. Since then, Lauren has been back and forth between her lives in England and Australia and has remained in friendly touch, with us both since I met Mike

It was a different story with Stefan, now married to Kim and with two small boys, Josh and Oli. He was running an extremely successful business, doing very nicely indeed and living in a very posh part of Surrey! (Only minutes away from Mike's sister Betty, who looked after them both for a while, but that's a chapter of the story we won't go into here. Honestly, if they made a film of this you wouldn't believe it!) Anyway, Stefan would get any news of Mike's life from Lauren, but there'd been no contact between father and son. Then, one day, Josh had asked his father: "Where's your daddy, daddy?" Now, what these kids want, they get! (Kim's father had died when she was a young teenager, so no granddad there; Stefan's adoptive father had split from his mother years ago, so none there either. If they wanted a grandfather, it came down to Mike.) So an evening with Lauren and Stefan with us in Canterbury was arranged (just before we came to France this year). It went extremely well, considering the background history. Four hours of food and drink and revelations and family tales went by very quickly, at the end of which we all seemed pretty happy with each other. So much so that he brought Kim and the boys down to meet us while Lauren was there, and we spent an interesting week discovering a whole new branch of the family.

At the beginning of September most of southern France, but initially the Gard and Hérault *départements*, had the most tremendous rains – in one night it rained as much as in one year in Paris – causing terrifying floods and deaths, after the River Gardon burst its banks. *"Le Sud Se Noye"* (The South Drowns) was the headline in Paris Match. Over thirty people died. It was declared a national disaster and a fund was started by the government. Returnees/friends, Roger and Gill, staying at La Clède for the fourth time, tried in vain to go to Nîmes *après le deluge*; all roads around it were closed. A couple of days later, we had to go that way ourselves to pick up Clare from the airport (Ryanair fly Stanstead to Nîmes). We could hardly believe our eyes – the devastation was dreadful. The floodwaters had receded, but cars that had been washed off the roads, some with their drivers, ended up in huge piles in the middle of fields. The vines were flattened horizontal; huge parts of the road were gone. One of the sorriest sights was a gutted garage, all pumps torn up, a pile of cars – with a boat on top! – and the owner sitting outside, on what had been the forecourt, surrounded by all his furniture and household stuff drying off. When we returned around 11pm, he was still there, sitting so dejectedly with one solitary camping gas light for company. Our hearts went out to him and to all who suffered so badly.

After Clare came Betty and Dru, Mike's sisters, for their second visit to the Ardèche. The weather was hot and sunny. We went up to Jeff and Renée's place to help with their *vendange,* and Dru bravely had a swim in the pool – the water was 19°C, not unusual for mid-September. Picking grapes may sound romantic, but it's actually very hard work. It's only because J-F & R have so few vines, that we consider it! Pressing them is much more fun, though equally hard – a lot of brute force is needed to turn the press – men's work really. Then we all celebrate drinking the freshly squeezed juice, which is delicious and does you a great deal of good. Don't drink too much, though. *"Ça purge!"* they all say, clutching their stomachs and laughing. (It goes straight through you!)

Friends, John and Mavis were in Barcelona – on their boat, and they rang and asked us if we'd like to visit – they were there until the end of September. Oh no, not likely! As soon as we had some free time, we were off! Their boat, *Ambition,* was moored in Port Olímpic, part of the new sea front development occasioned by the Olympic Games in '92. Staying on a boat would certainly be novel and a lot of fun, and parking in the port was a breeze – and cheaper, since John had a mooring there. Once on board, we all sat up in the cockpit having a drink and absorbing the heady atmosphere (heady for us, anyway – John and Mavis were more *blasé* and a tad jaded, having sailed up from Gibraltar that summer). It was mesmerising – like waterscapes are – watching all the comings and goings of the sailing fraternity and admiring the bold and dynamic new architecture, the twin towers, the enormous, copper-coloured fish sculpture behind us. We couldn't wait to get out there and explore what promised to be another spectacular city.

"Well, there's this geezer called Gaudí, whose name keeps cropping up everywhere," said John drolely. We laughed. "It's Gaudí International Year, but I think you either love him or hate him".

We both love Gaudí and we loved Barcelona with so many examples of his unique work! What was he on? Creative geniuses are nearly always out on a limb. First thing next day, we all headed for Park Güell, which started out as an exclusive housing development for private clients of his. The full commission to build an English-style garden city with sixty one-family houses was never completed. Only two of these were built in the end, the architect himself living in one. It's now a public park – "an architectural space which exists in communion with nature" – and looks rather like Disneyland, though a thousand times more exciting than that for me, but with just as many tourists! The originality and scale, the shapes and colours – all that mosaic – we were converted immediately and vowed to start collecting broken crocks and build a seat as soon as we got home!

You have to go see the *Sagrada Familia*, of course, started by Gaudí in 1883. Will this amazing temple ever be finished? It's the most incredible example of his surrealist imagination, with its eighteen sandcastle-like, parabolic towers, looking as if they'd dripped like stalactites from above, and detail and carvings on every surface. And that's just outside! Again, we walked and walked, gawping at magnificent buildings everywhere. More Gaudí at the Milà House – "*La Pedrera*", and the two adjacent houses Amatller and Battlló; the enormous squares, *Plaças del Rei* and *Catalunya* and *Plaça Reial* with Gaudí's fabulous wrought-iron streetlamps; the art district of *Carrer Montcada*, with its aristocratic residences now housing galleries and museums, like the unforgettable Picasso Museum; the cathedral and the *Palau de la Musica Catalana*, whose decoration inside and out is just exquisite. Even the tourist beats were fun, like the other new harbour, Port Vell and *Las Ramblas*, with all its souvenir stalls and brilliant mime artists, and Miro's mosaic, *Pla de l'Os*. Watch out for the tricksters, pickpockets and con-artists though! We saw them in action.

We went to the indoor market to buy delicious things to eat and couldn't believe the variety of produce on the many stalls (some over forty metres long) of fruit, vegetables, fish and seafood. What a treat for the eyes and tastebuds! Some of the city areas were obviously slum borderline, but in the streets, nearly everyone seemed in a good mood, as they strolled happily around in the sun, or sat in the cafés, indulging in *tapas* and people-watching.

Such a great atmosphere created by the Catalans, and so different from our experience with the Basques last year. Port Olímpic was edged on three sides by countless bars and restaurants, in one of which we had a truly wonderful *paella* this time. Less keen were we on the loud, bass-pumping music, which started up around 11pm as the nightlife got going and boomed until the small hours across the marina. Though we all were drawn like magnets to watch the pole-dancers, once back on board we didn't get much sleep!

We came home, after three days of avid sightseeing, via the Costa Brava and the beautiful coast road between Spain and France. I went to Tossa when I was about nineteen, and it was all Watneys Red Barrel, Tea Like Mother Makes and Fish'n'Chips then, as was its neighbour Lloret. Lloret seems to have just got worse, but Tossa's gone much more upmarket now, full of elegant restaurants specialising in Sunday lunches for the French, and has become a centre for scuba-diving. The coastline with its idyllic coves is much how I would imagine the Riviera was before all those villas were built. Long may it stay that way. It's a bit of a no-man's land, so it just might. We stopped for a drink and a breather in Pezenas in Languedoc. It's a pleasant, gentrified town to amble around, with its inevitable rather suspect art galleries and expensive *Antiquités* and *Brocantes*. We didn't take to its 'speciality', though – *Les Petits Pâtés* (like poor man's mince pies), apparently introduced by Lord Clive of India.

More drain digging, I'm afraid, when we got back, to get rid of the rainlake that accumulates at the cellar doors when it pours down. It's funny how, whenever we say we'll just ... (do something), thinking it will be easy, it never is! It took one awful lot of deep digging to get a pipe to a point where the water could run out – halfway down the entrance ramp in fact – a distance of about ten metres or more. But we persevered and were like delighted children when it next rained, running out in the middle of the storm to see if it worked, and it did! When it stopped raining, we decided while we were at it, we'd have another go at widening our entrance ramp a bit more. Although it was nearly 2m wide, it didn't look it, and some of our guests were still finding it very un-user-friendly.

There were plenty who didn't find it a problem, of course. Like Mike, for starters, driving up the huge van he hired when he came to do the roof. We've also had Volvo estates, Range Rovers, exotic sports cars, even a Cadillac, which the driver reversed up. (I can do that in my Renault!) Some tried it "only once" and said "Never again!" But the only person who's ever actually driven off the edge was my ex-husband, who having patronisingly taken the wheel of my Mini, saying I'd be bound to, promptly did it himself!

The problem with the widening was that we'd intrude into the alley, which was *commune* property, though not a way-through for cars, which we knew, of course, but which was all Christian would commit himself to telling us, when we asked him how much we could extend it. He shrugged and waved vaguely. They can be pretty cagey sometimes! So we just got on with it. Half-way through, his brother Alain shows up to see what we're doing. *"Faut pas faire ça,"* he said. (You Can't Do That!) *"La commune va le démolir."* (They'll take it down.) We didn't think they would, but it worried us and we took it back a bit. It ended up about 20cms wider, but we were still doubtful guests would find it any easier. So Mike attacked the corner of the terrace wall with his vicious scrutch hammer to gain further vital centimetres! We pointed the wall at the side and filled in some dips in the ramp itself. It looked much better. Compliments from all the Balazucs when it was finished, though Christian said: *"J'aurais pris un peu plus."* (I'd have taken more.) Don't you just love 'em?!

We'd been talking for a while about staying longer in Ribes and the need for better heating our side, if we did. We both fancied a wood-burning stove to go in our chimneybreast, but there was one major problem – no chimney! I chastised myself for not having made provision for it when Mike did the roof, but our futures weren't decided then, and I never intended to stay over the winter. Now it would require quite a large investment, a lot of work and make a great deal of mess.

According to new fire regulations, the stovepipe, if not in a chimney, had to be the expensive, double-insulated kind, even though it would be way out of reach, once installed up the wall behind. We were thinking we could get radiant heat from an un-insulated pipe, which would help heat the whole house, but this would annul any insurance, we were told. We'd also need an awful lot of this pipe, too. To get a good draw for the chimney, we'd have to go up over 10m, above our neighbour's roof on the extended wall. We umm-ed and ah-ed and couldn't decide, so it was put on the back burner! We ended up staying for Christmas and New Year, without installing the wood stove and having heard that in December 2001 there'd been snow and temperatures as low as –6°C. We would take our chances, but we were rather apprehensive about being warm enough.

But what a delightful surprise December 2002 was – it stayed mild, with a mix of sun and rain, but sometimes it was as hot as 28°C on the terrace in the lunchtime sun. We had to dress for the cold each morning. The answer was lots of layers, peeled off as the temperature rose in the sun, and replaced in the evenings, as soon as it dropped below the mountain. Having tarted up the front entrance, we thought we'd tackle the two rear ones, which exited on the top road at each end of the property – one a ramp and one a set of stone steps. We extended these steps higher and made new flowerbeds beside each entrance, ready for planting with shrubs the following spring. Breaking rocks in the hot sun sounds more like activity for convicts, but it's a real pleasure for both of us to do jobs like landscaping when the time's right. The soil's very manageable, the rocks are numerous, and there's no pressure; we can just create. The wider landscape around us changed completely, too, with no leaves on the trees – they were usually still there when we left in November. Now we could see so much more, discovering outlines we hadn't been aware existed, and enjoying the different light and colours of the winter countryside.

It was very Christmassy – the villages, shops and houses were decorated – the baubles and tinsel appeared, and we were like kids yet again, buying fairy lights for the terrace and balls for the tree. How about this for the ultimate in recycling?! It was finally time for the last part of the cat bush to go. We beheaded it with some ceremony and discovered that the ears made two perfect little Christmas trees. So we had one inside with red and silver balls and red lametta; and one outside, sprayed silver and gold with red bows tied on – this seemed to be the traditional local decoration. ("One 'ere on the terrace and one 'ere in the fireplace," as Mike so wittily put it!)

Christmas shopping was a real pleasure. Mike headed to Aubenas for my prezzies, I to Les Vans for his. It was bustling and festive, but easygoing – no real crowds in the shops. We thought about the usual shopping frenzy that greeted us every Christmas in Canterbury and sighed contently at the peace and joy of it all. The *metéo* was predicting a fine Christmas Day – *Noël au balcon,* they call it. This had been one of Peg's fantasies – to experience Christmas lunch outside on her French terrace – but she and Alan had never stayed in Ribes beyond October. We were very much hoping that we'd be able to do this for the first time.

A mild winter sun greeted us when we opened the shutters at around 9am, and it got warmer as the morning progressed. Our neighbours were up and about, preparing for a huge family get-together at noon – it would probably last for hours. I called out to them from the terrace.

"Bonjour, nos chers voisins. Joyeux Noël à vous tous!" *"De même,"* they chorussed. *"Fait beau, hein? Qu'est ce qu'on est bien ici."* (Same to you. Nice day! Great here, isn't it?)

"C'est parfait! On a de la chance." (It's perfect. We're so lucky.)

"Oui, il va faire chaud même." (It's going to be hot.)

"On va déjeuner dehors. Il nous faut une photo; personne n'va nous croire!" (We're going to have our lunch out here. We'll need a photo; no-one 'll believe us!) Christian grinned up at us from the alley. *"On a fait pareil il y a quelques années, mais on a trop de monde cette fois."* (We were able to do that one year, but we've got too many people coming today.) He called Mike down and motioned him to follow to his precious wine cellar, where he kindly presented him with a bottle of his favourite white *Viognier* to have with our meal.

"Allez. Bon appetit!" He waved as he went inside. *"Appellez-moi quand vous voulez une photo, OK?"* shouted Orane, his younger daughter. (Just call when you want a photo) *A plus!"* (See you later.)

They called us over to share *les desserts* – all six of them. And they'd already had six courses! This is a traditional Ardechois Christmas lunch, (12.00 – 18.00hrs), all home-produced once upon a time:

Le jambon cru avec beurre et olives	Raw (Parma) ham with butter and olives
Le saucisson	More raw ham in sausage form
Les asperges sauce verte	Bottled asparagus in herb sauce
Les bouchées à la reine	Chicken and mushroom *vol-au-vents*
Le civet de lièvre	Jugged hare
La dinde en terre	Baked turkey (usually with truffles)
Les cardons à la crème	Creamed cardoons (green veg)
Les haricots verts au beurre	Bottled green beans
Les picodons bien affinés	Mature goat cheeses
La bûche de Noel à la crème de marron	Christmas log with sweet chestnut *purée*
La crème anglaise	Custard, made with eggs
Les truffes au chocolat ou les marrons	Chocolate truffles or sweet chestnuts *glacés* preserved in sugar
Les oreillettes et les fruits secs	Small sugared 'doughnuts' and dried fruit

In these more affluent times, the first two courses would more likely be oysters and *foie gras*.

We were planning a very simple lunch for ourselves: *Dinde aux*

---

* This prompts me to relate a tale that went into the Anderson family repertoire. Some friends of friends from Yorkshire visited Peg and Alan once, and they all went out to dinner one evening and chose to eat the modest standard menu. First course: *soupe du jour*, brought in a tureen to the table and left there while you helped yourselves. After a while it would be picked up and taken to another table. This didn't happen and Donald happily continued to rehelp himself, declaring when it was empty, in his broad, Yorkshire accent, "Ay, I 'ate waste!"
Second course: *Truite aux amandes*.
"What's that, Alan?"
"Trout with almonds"
"Fish wi' nuts! By 'eck, I've never'ad fish wi' nuts before!"

marrons à la sauce forestière (Turkey with chestnuts[*] in a wild mushroom sauce) – out of a jar! – most French pre-prepared meals are pretty good – because we wanted to enjoy present-giving and the sunshine, and had *amuse-gueules* to make for the planned evening do with the Balazucs. But we had crackers and jokes and silly hats. Lucky joined us, of course – she has an extremely heightened sixth sense as meals appear on tables and she's spoiled rotten by the guests. We made her a tinsel collar and gave her a bit of turkey – of course! The temperature climbed to 24°C in full sun. We drank a toast to Peg and Alan – of course. Here we were again, fulfilling another of her dreams.

We'd invited our favourite neighbours to come over that evening for *vin chaud* (mulled wine) and mince pies, amongst other things. *"Qu'est'ce que c'est, mince pie?!"* This was the standard response when we introduced them to any 'foreign food' – carrot cake, chilled cucumber soup and curry with our own fig chutney come immediately to mind. The women were usually curious, the men suspicious, but they tried things cautiously and sometimes we made a real hit – on this occasion it was to be the houmous dip – home-made with lots of garlic – and served with tortilla and parmesan chips, which they'd never tried; and in fact, the mince pies went down quite well too. It was altogether a perfectly lovely first Ardèche Christmas.

On Boxing Day we were invited up the mountain to Roger and Pat's place in Laboule. They live in a most beautiful spot, near the top of the Tanargue range, surrounded by chestnut and pine woods (with boars!), a tinkling stream and their very own meadow. Roger built their house with the help of their four strapping sons, and Pat mucked in wherever needed. There were ten of us around the table at this English Christmas party. (We normally steer clear of 'Brit Club' do's, but it was Christmas after all.) It was interesting to meet new people who live in the area and to find out a little of their histories. We were asked three times by different couples whether we were 'integrated', to which I replied, "I certainly hope so after nearly forty years!" (Well, it's all a game of oneupmanship, isn't it?! In fact, I did meet a man at another of these do's, who'd been in the Ardèche three years longer than I!)

133

It was all very jolly and got more and more boisterous as the courses passed and the wine flowed, with regular cries of "*La parôle à .."* whoever had a joke or story to tell. There were loads of yummy desserts (the English excel at these – comfort food to counteract the disappointment we're all weaned on?) Hard to resist, when you really shouldn't eat any more. As for booze, four glasses of wine with food (and lots of water) are absolutely my limit, and Mike hardly drinks much, another bonus. So we made it safely down the mountain around 6pm, having had a very merry time.

New Year's Eve was a much quieter affair with just the two of us and a video or two for light entertainment. We hadn't planned to stay so late in France, but our tenants back in Canterbury were waiting for a house to be built, and it wasn't going according to schedule. We were told by our agent that they wished to keep the house on until 15 January, so we'd planned to stay in Ribes until the 7th, then spend a week travelling around like gypsies seeing friends and family, until we could move back in. On 2 January, we were informed that they'd moved out the day before! That's tenants for you!

On 5 January, it snowed. A very light shower, but it was the first time we'd ever seen snow on Ribes soil. It was getting decidedly colder and we decided to leave. As we climbed north over the mountain ranges, the snow got thicker and deeper. The French are pretty unused to this white stuff in the south and were obviously very unnerved by it, judging by the way they were all driving – at around 20kph! It wasn't an easy journey and we were glad for once to get back to our other home. It wasn't going to be a terribly long stay. Mike's daughter, Louise and her partner Lawrence were getting married – in Las Vegas! And we – that's fourteen family and friends – were all going too. And the war against Saddam was brewing ...

The trip to Vegas was better than expected. We thought the wedding at the Little Chapel of Flowers would be horribly tacky, but it wasn't at all. Quite charming, in fact, but I was the only one who cried. The wedding dinner at Caesar's Palace was expensive, but faultless. The architecture on The Strip is brilliant in places.

BACK TO THE GARDEN (2002)

We had another excellent meal at the Paris, and didn't have to queue for once, as the Yanks were boycotting it because of the war! (France refused to take part in it.) I went back time and time again to watch the fountains to music in front of The Bellagio (the classiest hotel) – the best free show in town. We went to a rock photography exhibition at the Rio, "Five Decades of Attitude" – apparently we were the only visitors for days, and they were so pleased to see us, they let us in for free. "Vegas isn't a cultural place," said the young guy on the door!

We went downtown. The old Vegas, the cab driver told us, had to be seen; it "had history"! – not even a century! It wasn't the greatest of areas, obviously playing second fiddle to The Strip, but the laser show wasn't bad. The helicopter trip to the Grand Canyon was the best fun of all, with lovely Joe, the pilot, who'd been in Vietnam at age 19, and now so disheartened at being on stand-by for Iraq. We stayed at the Flamingo Hotel[*], the original casino, courtesy of exceedingly unpleasant gangster, Bugsy Siegel. There's a shrine to him in the garden! I think that sums the place up really – one huge folly, and it's the fastest growing city in the States. God help us!

---

[*] We really confused them at Reception with the family names. Another strange coincidence: Louise Kay became Mrs Lawrence Bevan. Mike, therefore, suddenly had two Mrs Bevans in his life - and of course there were other Kays and Bevans in the party!

- 9 -
THE BIG HEAT (2003)

ON 9 NOVEMBER 1963, seven people were present and seated in the office of Maître André Méjean, the *notaire* of Joyeuse: Maître Méjean himself, Raymond Guérin, the agent acting for my mother, Henri Raynaud and his two sisters plus husbands, Germain and Marie-Louise Vamin, and Louis and Henriette Matal, the surviving inheritors and vendors of La Clède. The *notaire* read out the *Acte de Vente*. Then one by one, they signed their names. The *timbre fiscal* (stamp duty) was 5FF.

A few months short of forty years later, Mike and I left Canterbury on April Fools' Day and caught the afternoon ferry from Portmouth to Caen where we stayed overnight. Loaded as usual, we were taking our time over the journey. We got to Brioude (under three hours from home, but by five o'clock we'd had enough driving). Besides, we knew a smashing place to stay. The Hotel de la Poste was having new rooms built and renovation work done for the summer season, and all they had to offer in our price range, they said, was a 'modest' suite in the old annexe for 27 euros! Four rooms and a bathroom to ourselves, furnished as if from a *brocante*, but perfect for our needs! Plus, a wonderful dinner, we knew, to come.

Menu du Jour @ 13 euros – five courses – all beautifully cooked: Leek and potato soup (a surprise starter to whet the appetite), quiche and salad, roast farm chicken and Basmati rice, magnificent cheese selection (plus walnuts) and a choice of six desserts (or a small piece of each on one plate (Mike's favourite, which we remembered from another visit!) We don't have huge appetites and often avoid having a menu meal, as we find even four courses *de trop*. But we were familiar with the cuisine in this friendly, family-run hotel and knew we wouldn't feel bloated. (We declined second helpings, nevertheless!) Two sisters have inherited the business from their parents; one is the house and restaurant manager, the other the chef, a member of the *Association des Restauratrices*. We couldn't fault it in any way, and told them so.

In the Ardèche valley the weather was mild, but the house chilly. The weather got warmer, the house temperature stayed resolutely at 14°C. Even with heating, the stones take a while to warm up after being left unoccupied for the coldest winter months. But outside in the shade, on 18 April, the thermometer hit an unbelievable 32°C! Work in the garden dominates when we first arrive. Days are spent weeding and pruning – just generally tidying it up after the months of neglect. It had been dry for a couple of months, we were told, and we had had, as we usually do, some deaths in the garden. Whether from drought or frost, it's hard to say from reports from the neighbours. Versions vary so – the weather is a very subjective subject, it seems, and everyone tends to perceive it differently!

I was determined this year to do more with our modest three olive trees, particularly since Alain Balazuc had teased me that I only had them for decoration! They must be about fifteen or so years old now. Until last winter we'd never tasted the fruit, as we weren't there for the harvest around the end of the year. We always told Serge to take whatever olives were worth taking, and I'd always thought he tended and pruned the trees – they were planted while Peg and Alan were still alive – and we continued the arrangement. Mike and I had realised that pruning was obviously not taking place a couple of years ago, as the trees were growing quite tall and in somewhat contorted shapes. Last winter, when we stayed into January, we picked our olives and put them in storage jars in strong brine for six months (on Tony from Perth's advice). Over the winter in UK, I also read with pleasure Caroline Drinkwater's *The Olive Farm* [*] and Annie Hawes' *Extra Virgin* [**]. I vowed to seek help on olive tree husbandry when I got

---

[*] *The Olive Farm* by Caroline Drinkwater (Abacus, 2001). She was doing an author's evening at Waterstone's in Canterbury in early April, to launch the second part of her trilogy, but unfortunately we'd already left for France.
[**] *Extra Virgin* by Annie Hawes (Penguin, 2001)

to Ribes.

Mike and I were discussing the olive trees up on the highest of our garden terraces where they grow. Our neighbour above, Pierre, ever curious, came over to see what we were up to and have a chat.

"*Salut, Pierre. Ça va?*" we asked, almost in unison. "*Pierre, tu connais quelqu'un qui peut nous conseiller comment tailler nos oliviers?*" (Do you know someone who can advise us on pruning our olive trees?) Pierre always knows a man who does – he seems to know everyone.

"*Mais vous avez bien choisi le moment de me demander. Il faut le faire maintenant.*" (This is a good time to ask – it's time to prune now.) "*Samedi prochain y'a une demonstration de taille. Rendez-vous à la Salle Polyvalent à deux heures.*" (Next Saturday there's a demonstration on pruning olive trees. Meet at the village hall at two o'clock.)

We turned up at the appointed hour. There was an impressive turn-out of around fifty people, even a few women! We hung around for the obligatory waiting period – things very rarely start dead on time. Then the signal cry went up: "*Bon, on y va?*"

A cavalcade of some twenty cars started back up the hill. After about only 500 metres or so, the leaders pulled over and got out! We all followed suit, parking *n'importe où,* and walked *en groupe* into an olive grove at the side of the road.

There was much more greeting, shaking of hands and *bonhomie* going on, so typical of such occasions, particularly in rural France. We spotted a Balazuc family member, Eric, one of Christian's brothers, who'd been driving past, seen the crowd and come to check out what was going on. There was another jovial man, who greeted us. We knew his face, but couldn't quite place him. I spoke briefly to a young woman with a camera, who was covering the event for the local journals. Then our teacher, a small, wizened old guy, appeared, brandishing secateurs and pruning shears. After a brief introduction, he launched with enthusiasm into his first tree. Has anyone seen the movie Edward Scissorhands?![*] After a few

---

[*] *Edward Scissorhands* starring Johnny Depp (Twentieth Century Fox, 1990)

minutes, there was more of the tree on the ground than on the tree! It was hard to keep up, but generally he appeared to be cutting off virtually everything from the middle of the tree and any small branches which crossed or touched each other, plus any tips that were too high or that had suffered damage from the cold over the winter. At first, the entire audience was quiet, the odd camera snapped, including my own, but we just watched, as you do, concentrating hard. At the second tree, conversations started up again – questions, personal experiences coming from every side. Already a competitive faction had started up on the first tree – a brief seminar on grafting! We watched some more, became familiar with the pattern. "Let's go," said Mike. "Let's go and do ours while it's fresh in our minds."

We waited for a pause in the proceedings. After the third tree I approached our demonstrator. *"Merci bien, Monsieur, pour toutes vos astuces* (tips). *On va chez nous pour le faire toute de suite."* (We're going to go and do ours straight away.) He gave me a broad smile.

"Ça va? Vous avez compris? Vous pouvez vous débrouiller maintenant?" (Think you'll manage now?) *"Ah oui, merci. On n'en a que trois, vous savez! Mais on veut les bien entretenir quand-même."* (We've only got three but we want to look after them.)

We shook hands warmly, *"Allez, au revoir, Monsieur, au revoir tout le monde. Et bonne continuation!"*

We drove home, changed and realised we'd have to work fast before the rain which threatened. It had been forecast for Easter Sunday, but already grey clouds were looming and there was a strong south wind, which usually brings us wet weather. "OK, half an hour per tree he reckoned," said Mike. "Let's get cracking!"

And indeed, around ninety minutes later, just as we felt the first drops of rain, we'd finished and were well pleased with the results. The trees were a much better shape and seemed both more managed and manageable. Pierre came over to watch as usual. I thanked him for his help in putting us on to the event.

"Vous en avez trop taillé!" he said (You've taken too much off.) *"Ça m'étonnerait qu'il y en ait une bonne douzaine d'olives sur vos arbres cette année!"* (If there's a dozen olives on your trees this year,

I'll be amazed.) *"On copie ce qu'on a vu,"* I laughed. (We're only copying what we saw.) *"On verra."* (We'll see.)

We left and just got inside before the downpour started in earnest.

I think that was the last time it rained! Actually, it wasn't; it just felt like it. Like last year, June was uncharacteristically hot – temperatures in the shade reached 38°C. It got even hotter in July. Since we'd arrived at the beginning of April, it had only rained four times. It was good rain, not violent, so it didn't just run off the surface, but it wasn't enough to penetrate the soil very deeply. We had to save water. Gunhi had tipped us off that there were plastic barrels available at the *décheterie* (dump) in Joyeuse. We went there more or less as soon as she told us, as containers are suddenly very popular and hard to get hold of. We bought three for twenty euros – they hold around 180 litres each. *"'Y'en a encore?"* I asked the very nice man in charge. (Are there any more?) *"Oui, mais on doit les nettoyer. Venez demain. Combien il vous en faut?"* (We've got to clean them. Come tomorrow. How many do you need?)

"Encore six."

"Oui, ça marche."

"Super. A demain, alors. Salut."

The next day I drove the van back to the dump. I wasn't going to miss out on this. We desperately needed to store water and had cleared out a space under the front terrace to house the containers. The same pleasant guy helped me load up the van, but we had a job getting them all in – I'd gone on my own to save space and had one on the passenger seat. We'd just managed to close the back doors, when I spied a double plant pot stand in red wrought iron outside the 'shop'[*]. *"C'est combien, ça?"* I asked, pointing to the stand.

"Cadeau," he replied with a big smile, picking it up and succeeding in finding a place in the front to house it.

---

[*] They're allowed to sell anything worthwhile that people bring in, at moderate prices. You'd be amazed at what can be found there. I once bought a colour television for 200FF, which lasted three years!

"C'est très gentil, merci beaucoup."

We shook hands, or rather he preferred his wrist, on account of his dirty hands, which is the done thing here, even though we'd both been doing the same job! I was extremely pleased with my 'present'. Something else to clutter up our terrace, whose decor is red and white, an extension of the colour scheme in the kitchen. And I needed a home for a red and white amaryllis I'd just potted, a present from Mike's sister, Betty.

The heat continued, and continued. While Mike was away in England helping Clare with her flat, there were two couples in the *gîte* who'd returned for their fourth visit. They always came at this time of year, so they knew how hot it could get, but the weather was usually more varied in June. The river was low because of the lack of rain and had consequently lost some of its charm. It was almost too hot to work up the enthusiasm to go anywhere. We all agreed it was more like Africa than France, as we lay sweating, despite fans, in our hot bedrooms, trying to sleep at night. However, they had two classy sports cars with them, both with air-conditioning, so in the end, they spent most of the time driving around looking at things and not getting out much!

The fourteenth of July – Bastille Day – passed with a splendid firework display in Joyeuse, though much as I enjoy fireworks, I think I would prefer the mayor to provide some decent toilets somewhere in the town and take the pressure off the cafés. (Public toilets in France are generally very low on the priority list!) It was also full moon that night – a huge, hazy, yellow one because of the heat. But the tides changed the winds, and the weather, and suddenly *la canicule* was gone. The sun was still there, but that cooling north wind reappeared. We could breathe again at least, until the heat built up once more. But when, oh when, would we get a good storm?

By the end of July, we'd had one sensational-to-watch rainstorm that lasted only an hour, so the ground was still dry underneath. Lauren was staying with us again, this time with a new man in her life, Nick from Johannesburg. Throughout their week-long stay, they tried their versions of ancient Aboriginal and Zulu rain dances and took the credit for the 3mm of water from the storm!

On a more practical level, Mike diverted the pipes from the *gîte* showers to run into our barrels, and we siphoned this off or carried it in buckets to the beds where the shrubs needed it most. Alan's chestnut tree wasn't happy, with serious die-back problems, but how do you water a tree that big in a drought? The whole water situation was getting extremely serious. Most of our neighbours' *sources* had dried up. We didn't have one – only metered water that was getting scarcer by the day. It was not looking good.

Our village reservoir was so low that the local water board had mediated in a deal between the mayors of Ribes and St André. This neighbouring commune higher up the mountain has far fewer inhabitants and summer visitors and more *sources,* so had agreed to give us some. We were still swimming in the river early morning, in preference to friends' pools, a half-hour car journey away. There wasn't much left in it, but it was cleaner two days after the rain, which always stirs it up. Further downstream at Rosières, where the campsites start in earnest, bathing had been banned because of pollution. The authorities didn't want an epidemic on their hands. I would imagine the local doctors and nurses were already very overstretched – as they are every year – as people don't take enough care of themselves and suffer from canoeing accidents, sunburn, alcohol and food poisoning and the rest. This is one of the darker sides of tourism, and not the responsibility of the owners of the campsites, of course. In most French *gîtes*, too, advice and information can be a bit thin on the ground and holidaymakers are left to their own devices.

"Je voulais habiter en France, pas en Afrique!" I'd wail to the neighbours. We tuned into the *météo* every night and cried out in dismay as we heard the fateful words yet again: *"Les températures caniculaires vont continuer".* The mornings were just about bearable, but in the afternoons, there were only two choices of where to put yourself – either in the polluted? water along with hundreds of other bodies, or inside the house (temperature around 27°C). Outside in the shade it was 40°C – that's over 100°F! With all the shutters closed and no daylight, it was a bit of a troglodit-ic kind of existence. Mike would watch the Tour de France, read

142

or siesta and I would sit at my computer and write this. At 6pm we'd emerge looking a bit bleary-eyed and do a tour of the garden to see if everything had survived the ordeal of the day's heat. We'd have an *apéro*, appreciate the slight drop in temperature and then start the watering ritual. Hosing vegetables only was allowed. We had to hump the buckets of recycled water to all the far-flung trees and shrubs. We did manage to keep most things alive and only had one or two deaths in the garden, but it was all very reminiscent of Gérard Dépardieu in *Jean de Florette*.[*] – and utterly monotonous into the bargain. "We should get a life," I'd say to Mike, as we pushed ourselves into watering mode, "but I just can't watch things die."

There's an old American country song called "Cool Water". Joni does a version of it on *Chalk Mark in a Rainstorm*. I'd sing it to myself as I carted buckets two at a time up and down the ramps:

"Tonight we pray for water
Cool water
And way up there
If you care
Please show us where
There's good water
Cool, clear water."

I told Ian what it was like, on the phone.

"We're talking serious drought here, then," he said. Indeed we were.

As none of the Balazucs wanted to swim, claiming the water in the Beaume was dirty, we didn't go to the river for our annual picnic with *les Belges*, but to Orane's new house. She was waiting for the floor and wall tiles to be done, before installing the kitchen appliances and sanitaryware. Everything else was finished, though, and was looking good. Mike made one of his apple cakes. We also took a tray of our tomatoes. We'd tried some unusual

---

[*] From books by Marcel Pagnol, two films directed by Claude Berri, (Renn/RAI-TV/DD/A2, 1986), *Jean de Florette* and the sequel *Manon des Sources* - highly recommended and providing much insight into the pre-affluence lifestyle, culture and mentality of the inhabitants of south-eastern France.

varieties this summer and had large and cherry versions, in yellow as well as red, and some extremely dark red, almost brown, ones with a lovely nutty flavour. Garnished with green herbs, it made a colourful spread.* We also had a lot of cucumbers, so we'd made sandwiches with one of the delicious loaves from our favourite *Boulangerie Eschalier* in Joyeuse – a *Céréales* (five cereals and different seeds – no one else was familiar with it!) Also a large jar of our own olives, which we'd bottled with herbs and garlic. The reaction from neighbours when presented with new fare is always interesting, but we were unprepared for the praise we received, especially for the olives. This was the most gratifying, as they do know their olives; all the other things were novelties to them, after all. But they kept on about the olives. Christian's brother, Eric, who's a cook, was particularly complimentary. He said they were the best he'd tasted and wanted the recipe! *Quel honneur!* We love it when that happens. We're not going to have many this year, though, on account of the heavy pruning and the drought.

More records were being set this hot summer with the *vendanges* (grape harvests), which normally start around the second week of September. Locally at Ruoms, the grapes were picked on 8 August! Nationally, they were the earliest harvests since records had been kept. There was a crisis finding pickers, as a large part of the French nation was still on holiday! This didn't affect Ribes, which started a week or so later. Here the vineyards are relatively small, and it's the extended family and friends who pick for each other. On 12 August, when we tuned into the France 2 news, we heard that a record temperature had been taken in Orange of 42.6°C! (It didn't sound high enough to me, considering how much everyone was complaining!) This was followed by a distressing item from hospitals around the country, as well as Paris, reporting that "1,500-3,000 people – mainly elderly – had died directly or indirectly from the heat." On a later programme, we

---

* I especially love to use these Rasta colours in my dishes - for effect and taste. It's also a good and simple general guide that if you eat fruit and veg that are red, green and yellow everyday - you'll have a great balance of vitamins.

were informed that there had been "30,000 more deaths over the same summer period than normally." Statistics can be juggled, political and media statistics all the more so. But we were seeing scenes of patients on trolleys in hospital corridors that we Brits are well used to by now, but which really shocked the French. People are predicting that their health service will end up like ours. Not good news for a nation of hypochondriacs!

The weather often changes after 15 August, I kept telling myself, even though there didn't seem to be any rules any more. And, following the full moon, we did have two big storms, with violent winds and a fair amount of rain – 12mm this time. Enough, anyway, to give us a day or two's break from watering. What bliss! We hardly knew what to do with ourselves! The following week the hot sun returned, but it was fresher. At least you could go out during the day. And we had to – an elderly neighbour had died, and we had a funeral to attend.

It was Rosy's mother, Lucie, who died, aged 91. Rosy, from Marseille, is a very special woman. She's tiny and energetic – seventy but looks at least ten years younger – and always cheerful. She has a holiday home in our hamlet and brings her mother every summer for a few months. (It was Rosy who adopted Min the cat.) I'd popped in to see them both quite a lot while Mike was away in England, to see if she needed some shopping – she had no car – or to keep her company for a while. Lucie, or Mamie as everyone called her, had had Alzheimer's for several years. In Marseille, Mamie would go to her *Club du Troisième Age* two days a week, but in Ribes, Rosy had no time at all to herself except when she'd put Mamie to bed. Mamie would say to me every time she saw me: "*Tu es magnifique*" and I'd reply: "*Non, Mamie, c'est ta fille qui est magnifique, et toi aussi.*" (Your daughter's the magnificent one, and you too.) Mamie had already fallen twice and Rosy had come to me for help. When it happened for the third time on the stairs, we needed Roberte's help too. She was thankfully on hand, watering her terrace pots when it happened. (It's very reassuring having an A & E nurse living opposite. We've made use of her professional services on several occasions.) Mamie wasn't badly hurt, thankfully, just a few bruises.

Rosy had finally managed to get a room for Mamie for a month in a nearby *Maison de Retraite,* which meant she'd get a much-needed break. Her son Jean-Louis came up for some holiday with friends from Marseille, and she was just beginning to *se décon-tracter* (relax). They visited Mamie every day, and Rosy came to tell us that the home was wonderful and her mother was very content. The next day she and Jean-Louis came round with very different news, that Mamie had died the night before in her sleep. (A wonderful way to go and a relief, but hard to say to the newly grieving. She knew anyway.)

The funeral service took place in Ribes rather than in Marseille, as that was where the 'family' was[*]. A few friends came up from the coast, and around thirty people gathered in the church *place* at 11am in the hot sunshine. Ribes church, originally built at the end of the 12th century and renovated in the 1950s, is a very particular shape, not at all like other village churches around here. It's listed for its frescos inside, though little of them remains, unfortunately. All the neighbours from our hamlet were there (except the Pansiers, who are Jehovah's Witnesses, and the Balazucs – all at work). Apart from the four staff of the *Pompes Funèbres* in pale grey-green suits, everyone else was casually dressed, some even in jeans. Not much black in sight (we wore half-black); no scarves covering female heads, though I took one just in case.

The informal service lasted about half an hour, with two hymns, two readings, sprinklings of incense and water over the coffin, and a short sermon. At the end, the pallbearers stepped up to the coffin, resting on a kind of trolley, and pushed rather than carried it out of the church. We filed out, following them into the cemetery, where we queued in the baking heat during a last prayer, before passing in front of the coffin to sprinkle more water and say our goodbyes to a wonderful old lady. No-one stayed for the burial, but left the graveyard to say their *condoléances* to Rosy and Jean-Louis at the gates. We had tight, emotional hugs with

---

* Rosy lost her husband some years ago, her other son two years ago, and Min the cat only a month before. For immediate family, she only has her son, Jean-Louis (and her other cat, Brunette) left.

both of them. I seemed to swamp Rosy who's about half my size.

"*Tu m'as aidé à la soulever,*" she smiled at me through her tears. (You helped me lift her up.) I was already a little tearful myself. "*Oui, ma chère Rosy.*" I kissed her on the forehead and hugged her some more, then turned to Mike and grabbed his hand. We headed sadly up the short road to the hamlet, catching up the other near neighbours, sharing weather talk with Mme Nicholas, whom we'd barely seen for weeks because of the heat, and Pierre, whose presence we're constantly aware of even if we don't see him much (see next chapter!) They're both regular churchgoers, though there's only one service a month now. Perhaps they like a good funeral as well. They're both into *troisième age* themselves and certainly seem to know everyone. In the cool of early evening we returned to visit the grave, now covered in flowers – ours were a simple bouquet of white lilies – and to sign the remembrance book outside the church.

At last the really heavy heat went away, and by the last week in August we found we could work outside again in the mornings; the garden had been pretty much neglected apart from the watering. Mike was wanting something to do and decided to get on with the short path we'd planned to make to join his ramp to the steps down to the courtyard. We used to get a great deal of erosion when it rained heavily; water and sandy soil would pour down the steps at the side of the house. We'd managed to curtail a great deal by building up walls and steps and levelling terraces. This path was the final stage in our attempts to cut it down even more and divert the rainwater more usefully towards trees and shrubs. We'd been given some *lauzes* (*schist* flagstones) by Gunhi in exchange for some building work we'd done for her. These, mixed with a few coloured stones from the river, did the job very well indeed. Another great addition to the garden by Mike, it finished off his ramp legacy beautifully.

The last weekend in August – the school term began on 1 September – was the usual chaos on the roads, as an awful lot of northern European families made the trip back home. The village appeared to empty overnight. The shops suddenly went back to winter timetables and two to three hour lunch breaks, or closed all together as the proprietors left for their vacations. Some of our housemartins abandoned us as well. We watched them gather around the house – maybe the flock goes from site to site to pass on the message that's it time to be flying south. It was an amazing sight to see about fifty or more on the roof, clinging to the walls and swooping and diving around the courtyard in readiness for their trip. The temperature had suddenly dropped at night. It was only 13°C on the terrace in the morning. These extremes are quite a shock to the system; only three weeks ago, we'd still been sweating continuously! Now we would need to open the shutters for solar heat, rather than hide behind them. Still hot in the brilliant sun, but chilly in the shade, you never know quite what to wear!

In late May, we'd had a week's break in our bookings. That's all it takes and we're off to explore a new area! We went to Lyon then for a culture and horticulture fix at the *Musée des Beaux Arts* and the *Parc de la Tête d'Or*. We'd camped in a site just outside in St Genis for a mere ten euros (hotel rooms in the centre of Lyon were forty and upwards) and went into town with a *Liberté* ticket for use on buses, trams and *metro*. Afterwards, passing through Rhône-Alpes, we saw the longest (six kilometres) Roman *Aqueduc du Gier*, wandered around pretty villages like St Laurent d'Agny and eventually followed the river Loire back to its source on the Ardèche plateau. We found a brilliant place to camp, south of Le Monastier. We were on top of the world, in the middle of nowhere, with nothing but mountain ranges all around. Like two delighted kids, we snacked happily on wine and nibbles, watching the sunset. The next day, we drove along the winding mountain roads, past meadows of wild narcissi, and walked the five kilometres round the beautiful *Lac d'Issarlès*. In May, there was hardly anyone there; in July and August, its sandy beaches would be heaving with hot bodies. Just at the end of our circuit, we came upon and visited the former home of a clogmaker's family, now a small museum, built inside a large cave in the rockface beside the lake. It's just amazing what our forebears got up to and how they lived! We could use more people like them these days, with all their positive ingenuity. Necessity and invention are two words that come to mind – no-one in the 'developed' world needs anything anymore (except the latest DVD or mobile phone from the marketing men, of course. We're going soft in body and head!)

At the beginning of September, we had a second free week and were planning to take off north-west to the mountains. I met Rosy at the baker's van. She said she'd been at one of her favourite restaurants in Le Bez (at about 1,000 metres) for lunch the day before. She'd been cold – it was only 15°C at midday! – and we were advised to take trousers and sweaters with us on our short break of three days and two nights. We certainly needed them, even though the days were warm and sunny. We travelled through our favourite Lozère, via Langogne and its lake, into the *département* of Cantal (great cheese), to visit 'Tonton' Serge Balazuc, on his annual *cure* at the spa town of Chaudes Aigues (where the water comes out of the source at 82°C, the hottest in Europe). We were passing through a village called Termes, and the shape of its church, perched on the hilltop, caught my eye. There was an *auberge* on the roadside and it looked just our kind of place. We had a room for thirty euros and ate fantastically well for nine. The surrounding countryside's lovely and so rich in stone, they even made fence posts out of it! The next morning was cold; the grass looked frosty white, though it hadn't actually frozen. (Christian told us on our return that the same night at Lanarce on the Ardèche plateau, near Coucouron where he works, at around 1400 metres, the temperature had fallen to 0.2°C – on 3 September!)

We soon warmed up with *croissants* and hot *café au lait* sitting outside a bar in the early morning sun. We were heading for the *Viaduc de Garabit* – a huge iron bridge, built by Eiffel in 1882 over the dammed up river Truyère. The lake formed behind the dam is huge with mountains on all sides. It's stunning country in Cantal, and our easy drive on minor roads over the Margeride was a joy. Even more so, as we chanced upon another of France's thousands of *musées* – the *Ecomusée du Jardin* at Ruynes. Here we found the ruins of a *château*, complete with former dungeon in a tower, now an exhibition space all about the local 'industry' – *la moisson* (harvesting/gathering) of herbs, wild narcissi for perfumes, mushrooms and *myrtilles* (blueberries) – practised for centuries by the

locals. The castle walls now house a garden full of plant speci-
mens, all beautifully landscaped and well thought out to entertain
both kids and adults, with boxed information cards everywhere.
We were most impressed and said so to the young and enthusias-
tic curator. As we paid our four euros per head entry at the end, I
asked her about their finances and how easily they survived. They
were just managing to keep it going with the help of grants and
private sponsorship, she told us, but they had to work hard on
publicity and fundraising every winter to do so. I hope it lives on.
There was so much thought and energy going into it and into the
programme of events they organised. Happily, we weren't the
only visitors. A few other couples and a coachparty of *troisième
âge* (OAPs) seemed to enjoy their trip too.

It was lunchtime – time for one of our customary rituals on holiday – a picnic of today's choice of yummy things from a bakery.
God bless French bakers for offering so many delights, both
savoury and sweet – crusty, tasty breads, mini *pizzas* and *quiches,
croque-monsieur,* and those fruit tarts! And of course we all know
about the variety of cheeses* and fruit. The best ever takeaways.

We drove on through more beautiful countryside, stopping to
look at ancient villages like St Julien and Prades in the Allier
Gorges. We were heading for Lamastre, via Le Puy, back into
northern Ardèche. The next day we were going to Take The M
Train – *Le Petit Mastrou* – an early twenthieth century steam train
now belonging to the private *Chemin de Fer du Vivarais,* through
the Doux valley to Tournon.

Our second overnight stop was in nearby Désaignes, a pretty
little village. Both our hotel rooms this trip were no 9 – I love coincidences like that! The *Logis* looked good but wasn't – you win
some, you lose some. Same prices, big drop in quality. (Some parts
of the Ardèche, I have to say, can be pretty poor value for money.)
But if the hotel was disappointing, the train ride certainly wasn't.

Soon after our return, we had a glorious two full days of light
rain, which did the garden no end of good – it perked up consid-

---

* I believe de Gaulle once said something about the impossibility of govern-
ing a country that produced over four hundred and fifty different cheeses!

erably and suddenly things were in bloom again. This was followed by an Indian Summer (so soon after the 'normal' one!) and another week of *canicule* and watering. On our way back from our short holiday, going through Laurac, we'd noticed signs advertising an *été indien* at the *Relais Fleuri* restaurant (as seen on TV, owned by the mother of the estate agent who did the deal for Nippi and Nigel). Their fans may like to know, probably already do, that Nippi's – allegedly – opening an Indian restaurant near Vals les Bains, and that there's to be another series. We wondered whether he'd been doing some market research at the *Relais*, trying the locals out on a few dishes, before he committed himself to going solo! (See Update 2004)

We had our last river swim on 19 September. *L'eau était un peu fraîche*, as they say, but it was just lovely lying naked in the sun afterwards. For the next day and a half it rained – again, great for the garden, but that was the end of bathing for this year. Summer was well and truly over.

Louise, Mike's daughter came to visit us late October – on her own this time, *sans mari* – and we had a lovely week together. The weather was good. On one beautiful day we drove up the Drobie valley, taking two of the bikes in the back of the van – Mike and Louise were going to cycle back to Ribes. Just under halfway between Ste Mélanie and Sablières, there's an old mule-train path down to the river and *Le Pont du Rouge*, an ancient, possibly Roman, stone bridge, that links the two mountain paths on the route between Joyeuse and Sablières. It's a beautiful walk down through the *châtaigneraies* (chestnut groves) on the *schiste* walled terraces. The path itself is cobbled the entire way – it's an amazing human feat. The bridge is a perfectly simple, two-arch construction built onto the rocky sides of the river. The water's so clean and clear and full of fish, and there's a handy, sandy beach where we could picnic in the warm sun. Heaven!

After lunch we climbed back up, finding some large, choice chestnuts on the path (the only ones you're allowed, as visitors, to pick up) and filling our carrier bags. At the top, the bikes came out of the van, and father and daughter climbed on. I was driving the van back to Ribes to attend a meeting at the *mairie'*. "Last one home's a sissy," I joked, as I set off. "See you back at the ranch. Ride carefully, now."

The road goes gently up and down for part of the way back to the Beaume river, then it's downhill and level all the way, until ... the dreaded 2km uphill climb to La Clède! Louise excelled herself and did it in thirteen minutes! Mike did it too, just a bit behind her! Wussy me drove up, of course! That evening, Christian asked me how the meeting had gone.[*] "Ah, oui," I jokingly overenthused. "La démocratie en action, Christian, c'etait chouette!" Then, more realistically, I shrugged, smiling "Non, tu sais, la politique locale? Pas vraiment mon truc." (Local politics aren't really my thing.)

He looked relieved and laughed. "Moi non plus. Une grosse perte de temps à mon avis." (A big waste of time.) "Ils voulaient notre opinion, c'était tout – une formalité. J'ai un questionnaire pour toi. Ils veulent connaître notre avis! On peut les compléter ensemble?" I asked him. (They were just going through the motions of asking for opinions. I've a sheet for you to fill in – they want our advice! Perhaps we can do it together?)

"Oui, OK," he laughed. "Mais, c'était gentil, quand-même, de m'avoir invitée à la réunion." (It was nice to be asked to the meeting though.)

"Mais, pourquoi pas? Vous faites partie des meubles maintenant!" (Why not? You're part of the furniture now!) I smiled at him. What a lovely thing to say, I thought. I filled in my sheet; the pros outweighed the cons by a long way. Christian didn't do his, we found out over a roast boar dinner at their place later on that week. I wasn't surprised. He would be the first to admit he's a cynical man, but I didn't realise it went this far! He expounded his philosophy on life: "Tout le monde a ses merdes et s'en occupe. Tout le reste, c'est du cinéma!" (Everyone's got problems and gets on with sorting them out. Everything else is fantasy.)

"Alors, c'est chacun pour soi?" asked daughter Orane, dining

---

[*] I'd received a summons from the mayor to attend a meeting at the *mairie* on Tourism and the Future. Afterwards we were given sheets to fill in on the pros and cons of our village. (Christian had also had a summons, as he too had a gîte, but couldn't go - as the meeting was at 4pm and he was working.)

with us. (It's every man for himself, then?)

"*Oui,*" said her father vehemently. "*Oui et non,*" I added lightly. "*Ne crois pas tout ce que dit ton père. Il a dû passer une mauvaise journée.*" (Don't believe everything your dad says. He's just having a bad day.) "*Tous les jours sont mauvais pour lui!*" she retorted, laughing. (Every day's a bad day for him!)

Jean-Louis, Rosy's son, had a very bad day the next day. (They'd come up for *Toussaint*, the last holiday before Christmas of the French year.) Late afternoon, around dusk, we were inside and answered agitated knocks on the front door. It was a distraught J-L, in a dreadful state, explaining thirteen to the dozen how they'd been mushrooming up in the woods, they'd wandered apart and he'd lost Rosy. It was dark; she might have fallen. He'd looked and shouted, then decided to come back home, having called the *pompiers,* but they'd take a while to arrive. What could we do? We quickly donned coats and grabbed torches. We'd drive up the mountain and look, J-L would stay and wait for the *pompiers.* We were just writing down his mobile phone number by the van, when Rosy appeared out of the darkness, unharmed, carrying her large bag of mushrooms. Mother and son fell on each other, laughing and crying with relief, and vying to explain their versions of the drama. We laughed with them, in amazement as well as relief. She's really something, Rosy. Seventy, with a heart condition to boot, she'd simply found her way out of the woods in the dark and walked the three kilometres or so home. That's how she is and that's how well she knows all the paths!

Our season had ended late October when our last guests had left, by which time it had become decidedly autumnal. The leaves on the virginia creeper were now a deep red and falling continuously. It's the second of our favourite seasons here. The weather's mixed, but there are many sunny, hot days of anticyclonic weather, special to this south-eastern part of France. It's time again to prune, have bonfires and plant. We wanted to put in a hedge at the top of the garden, in an attempt, probably futile, to make a barrier between ourselves and Pierre's dogs' endless barking. Another outing, while Louise was still here, was to our favourite nursery to see what was on offer. We needed something that required very little water and grew fast, but we were definitely not *leylandii* fans! Our oracle, Madame Fournier, recommended *Eleagnus Ebbengei*, with silvery green leaves and fragrant white flowers in November. At least a dozen to cover eight metres, which @ 15 euros each for biggish plants was going to be a pretty expensive barrier! I couldn't resist, of course, and bought them. Louise, in the back of the van, sat in the middle of a forest on the way home.

"I thought we were just going to look!" she wailed, fighting for breath!

In November, we started our last house project for the year – for ever? Don't think so, knowing us! – a makeover of our bedroom. It was the last room in need of serious attention. We had to lower the ceiling and insulate against extremes of heat in summer and cold in winter. We purchased vast quantities of *lambris* (tongue and groove pine boarding) and *laine de verre* (Rockwool) *en promo*. We'd bought a lovely old, art deco bathroom set in white porcelain at a *brocante* in May, which comprised a wall light, shelf, soap dish and towel hook, and had then found a thirties-style *vasque* (vanity basin) at one of the DIY stores. Mike thought diagonal boarding would look good for the new ceiling.

"Oh, Mike," I groaned after the first few boards. "This is so complicated. Let's do it straight. It's going to take forever this way." This is like a red rag to a bull. We persevered, even though he too got some of the angled cuts wrong! It took two days longer, but was worth the extra effort. Painted white, it looks brilliant! As if this wasn't enough, he suggested a thirties-style unit – "a straight front will be boring" – with, guess what, diagonal tiling. Deco mad, he was! I left him to create this masterpiece himself, and concentrated on slurrying the walls white, that Serge had rough-plastered and I had painted years before. Then I sealed the exposed sandstones with a 50/50 mix of Unibond and water to help reduce dust, just as we'd done with the walls in the mezzanine. We repainted the cement floor black and relaid our large black and white rug. The final touch was a bidet, which I've always wanted. Now it's become almost a necessity, as foot maintenance is increasingly difficult due to age and a decline in athleticism – I can barely get my feet up into the new, higher wash-basin!

The zebra-pattern wool rug in the bedroom was another happy *brocante* purchase. We enjoy going to these, as we both like old stuff, and Mike's always collecting something! His latest is all things in bakelite. It's getting more *recherché* now, so the dealers are upping their prices, but he's had some great finds. This year he struck gold. A friend, Alain, whom we'd met through Jeff and Renée, decided to start up an antiques/*bric à brac* business. He spent all summer doing the rounds of the *marchés aux puces, brocantes and vide-greniers* (flea markets and carboot sales), which is a full-time job around here, on the hunt for stock. In the process, he found one or two gems for Mike – a deco clock and a fan (both work), a thermos, ashtrays and a big bag of electrical bits, like plugs and switches. We're fast running out of space – one niche in the lounge is devoted to the collection and it's full to bulging! Mike's favourite stalls are the ones where things are spread out and priced – *Tout à 10 euros*, for example, or those that have crates of bits and pieces to rifle through. I vaguely collect ducks and am a sucker for books and old albums. I once found a (rather battered) copy of Sticky Fingers by the Stones, with the original zip cover designed by Warhol, at a small fair in nearby Lachapelle for a mere two euros! (He wanted to be reassured, though, that I was a real Stones fan!) I see a lot of excellent sixties/seventies albums at these markets – I have many of them already – I guess because of all the *baba-cools* (drop-outs) attracted to the Ardèche at the time, so I have quite a field day, as well as a good dose of nostalgia.

I have a particular fond memory of one summer market in Joyeuse, which hosts two weekend antiques fairs a year. Browsing among the stalls, our two sets of eyes suddenly landed on the same thing. The stallholder had spread out his wares on the ground on a large black and white carpet. We approached and looked. *"Bonjour. Désolée, mais c'est pas vos marchandises qui nous intéressent, c'est le tapis!"* (We're really only interested in the rug!)

A look of great surprise and a laugh from the handsome young merchant. *"Vous avez un prix pour ça?"* I asked.

"Ben, oui!." He thought for a few seconds. *"Cent cinquante balles, d'accord?"* (£15) *"C'est bon."* We all smiled. I gave him the money. The carpet was rather dirty but not stained or worn. It could live again in our black and white bedroom. Perfect.

"Mais on ne va pas le prendre toute de suite! On fait un tour et on revient dans une heure, d'accord?" (We won't take it straight away! We'll come back in about an hour, OK?) *"Oui, OK, ça marche. A plus."*

We wandered on, and only a few minutes later, I saw something else I wanted. A carved wooden goose, about two foot high, in a rich, dark hardwood. I know I paid too much for it, but I love how it fits so well in our house (and makes such a handy hat stand!) And it always brings back the picture to my mind of the two of us wandering contentedly hand in hand through the sunny square back to the car with the rolled-up carpet on Mike's shoulder and me, the other hand round the goose's neck!

And so the major building and decorating work in our house is finally complete. It's taken us six years and it's just how I wanted it to look. I started it all in 1977; Mike has helped finish it, doing the lion's share always, and added many beautiful ideas and features of his own. It's given us both enormous satisfaction and pleasure, despite the size and, at times, unpleasantness of the tasks, and we're very pleased with, and proud of, the achievement – **our** home in the sun. Maybe we can now start living more like normal folk. Looking more presentable would be good for a start – we seem to have been living and dressing down forever. Even more embarassing when you live next to women who always look immaculate. Even when they're doing housework, gardening or painting, there's not a mark anywhere or a hair out of place! I daren't go out sometimes in case they see me on a bad hair day in my tatty work clothes! I can certainly empathise with Gemma Bovery, in her strip cartoon:[*]

"What's great about England – if you want to, you can go for days looking complete <u>crap</u> – and no-one notices. Here, you get

---

[*] *Gemma Bovery* by Posy Simmonds (Jonathan Cape, 1999). Marianne sent us this after her stay here. Thankyou, M, I treasure it!

looked at like you're seriously deviant ... The French <u>really</u> do believe in poncing up 24 hours a day. Exfoliating really is a national pastime[*] ... The <u>strain</u> of it! The <u>time</u> it must take them. Nauseating." !!

This has got me nicely into whinge-mode. I'm good at that – I could whinge for Britain!

---

[*] Orane is an itinerant beautician – this is pretty much all she does on her rounds!

- 10 -
NEIGHBOURS, EVERYBODY
NEEDS GOOD NEIGHBOURS

"CERTAIN HOUSEHOLDS in Ribes have been here for ten to fifteen generations during three or four centuries of working on the land. There have been small local industries, but everyone lived, in whole or in part, off the land. The local inhabitants no doubt have their faults, but also possess strong qualities, like patience and single-mindedness towards work. It's frightening to imagine the effort required by these rough workers to move so many stones, build so many walls, so they could plant their vines, olive and chestnut trees. The harshness of the work and the lack of resources made them a little on the mean side, not prone to excess, so they could survive and raise a family, look after their land and save a bit too. In short, a love of work and economy, with a spirit of tradition, common sense, pride, politeness, and mostly still religious – these are the characteristics of the locals." (Translated from *Notice sur la Paroisse de Ribes* written by Abbé V Etienne, 1944)

My parents, as the first foreigners to buy a house in the village, were overwhelmed from the start at the friendly welcome they received from *les Ribois*. They, especially Peg, since she could speak the language, put a lot into 'public relations', if you will, but they relished their acceptance and the time they spent with neighbours who became real friends. So do Mike and I. (We're still the only English here, and the language is certainly not widely spoken!) The Balazucs (cf family tree, p182), in particular, through three generations now, have always treated us like members of the family, inviting us regularly to their houses for drinks and meals and to all their *fêtes*. (We've actually gone into a fourth generation in 2003 with the birth of Vladia's baby Louna, with her partner, Ludo, in late February.) We are, however, and always have been, aware that we are the foreigners. We have invaded their space and, therefore, don't want to make any serious waves. We just try to blend in as much as possible. I'm sure the locals think us odd – nice, but odd! – but they're all so kind and are more than happy to help us with anything if we ask, which we rarely do (mainly because Mike seems able to solve pretty much anything). He's certainly impressed Christian – we both got such genuine big hugs from him when we left this year. And Christian and I go back forty years, so he must have a fairly good measure of me. *"Tu dis ce que tu penses, c'est bien, ça"* he's told me. (You say what you think. That's good.) Here goes!

First of the whinges – with apologies to all dog-lovers! We're in the heart of hunting country (actually, pretty much everywhere in France is hunting country!) Consequently, there are a lot of dogs around – they're part of rural France. They're part of urban France too – remember the dogmess police in Paris with their sucking machines? They've long given up getting on top of the problem! The thing is, in the country, most of the dogs aren't really pets as such and only get out on hunting days. The rest of the time they're penned in day after day and only see their owners at feeding times. Basically, they're all bored rigid and so, when anything moves, they bark – endlessly – day or night. These days there's more traffic of every kind in our corner of the village – more cars, whose drivers all stop to chat to Pierre behind us, more visitors, walkers (with or without other dogs), cyclists, mothers with prams (and sometimes dogs), local residents who do walk their dogs, with irritating results (see below!) France is full of dogs – eight million, apparently, as heard recently on French TV, though who's worked that one out and how, I can't imagine. I'd like to see them try to introduce licences here! Ribes is certainly full of dogs, particularly the hunting ones and the small, yappy ones kept as pets.

Pierre has hunting dogs – five this year. Two are getting on, he informed Mike and me when we arrived, so he'd bought himself another puppy over the winter. We tried to smile. It's a cute one, but we've grown to hate it! (It yelps, rather than barks, as if it's in pain.) Pierre is the eternal bachelor at 77 and still in pretty good shape, but hardly ever goes hunting these days, so his almost never go out. He's a good neighbour, despite his *"filles"*, as he calls them. We chat a lot and swop garden produce. He's a great source of information about all sorts of things and keeps a watchful eye on the place in our absence. He knows his dogs can be a nuisance and often shouts at them. I told him jokingly, when we were planting the new hedge, that it was our last-ditch attempt to get some peace! He laughed. There's nothing he appreciates more than a good wind-up!

Another neighbour, who visits at French holiday times, drives us nuts! Her regular, three-times-a-day walks around our hamlet with her three has become a bit like a Groundhog Day[*]-type nightmare. Not a lead in sight and pointlessly and continuously calling out instructions which they all ignore. Apart from the obvious drawbacks of doggie-dos to clear up – she and most French never would[**] – and frightening Lucky the cat out of her wits, they are led very slowly along the same route each time. Up past Pierre's house, where they set off his dogs; another thirty yards while they calm down. Then they turn and come past again, which sets Pierre's off again. She appears to be completely unaware of the noise and disruption caused by all this. Pierre, if he's in, just shouts at his and then carries on shouting down the phone, or shouting at other passers by – he's deaf and he knows everybody – while our and our guests' blood pressure rises, until peace and quiet is eventually restored – until the next time. Lovely village, shame about the dogs![***]

We have nine neighbours in and around our hamlet, *Le Chauvet*

---

* The film *Groundhog Day* (Columbia Pictures, 1993), starring Bill Murray and Andie MacDowell, has misanthropist weatherman Phil Connors reliving the same day over and over again, until he gets it right by being nice to people.

**For the first time ever in Joyeuse, this autumn, I saw a handwritten notice: *Veuillez ramasser les crottes de vos chiens* (Please pick up your dogs' mess). I obviously have one ally! Carrying a trowel and burying it would seem the obvious solution in the country.

***. One of Peg's well-used outbursts, in any conversation about kids' bad behaviour, was "It's not the kids, it's the parents." It's not the dogs, it's the owners!

(see plan pviii). The most recent, Anne, is very recent – she moved here only in September this year, from Lyon, where she still works part-time, so we haven't seen much of her as yet. We hardly ever saw her predecessor, who was rarely here. But Anne plays jazz piano and has already invited us out to a club, so it could be the start of a good friendship. Some new neighbours for my parents were less welcome. Peg and Alan arrived in Ribes in 1985 to find a concrete bungalow had been built a mere twenty-five metres in front of La Clède, almost entirely blocking their view of the village down below in the valley and, in particular, of the beautiful old stone *mas* and tower, the former *seigneurie* – one of the most attractive buildings in the commune. Christian had rushed out to greet them, seeing their incredulous expressions. Peg was in tears by now, Alan in shock.

"*J'ai fait de mon mieux pour l'empêcher*" (I did my very best to stop it).

In fact, the house was not strictly legal. The parcel of land was so small that the required distances from existing properties had not been met. But the mayor had allowed the construction to go ahead anyway. (I have to say I Suspect Foul Play since the mayor and the owner were related.) Christian had bought part of the property next to his from his neighbour, Albert Vermalle, so that the Balazuc household could be extended, but had not been able to buy the land that went with it. He went on to tell how Albert, originally from Marseille, had wanted to have a house built for (himself and) his wife – the sister of Mme Nicholas, another neighbour. (Rumour has it that he'd had an affair, his wife had stayed in Marseille with their son, and he had promised her, in an attempt to pacify her, a summer house in the village.) His son-in-law, a builder, had constructed this very un-'des res' very speedily over the winter. The house would only be occupied in July and August and would stand empty otherwise. (Wouldn't be much of a garden there then!) The following year, the whole of the centre of Ribes became a Stone Zone – any new building has to be built or clad in stone. Talk about shutting the stable door ...!

Roberte certainly wasn't any happier about the new neighbours either. The Balazucs avoid talking to the Vermalles! "*C'est tout à fait minable!"* (absolutely ghastly) was her brutal opinion of the bungalow, which is even closer to her house. One evening soon after their arrival, Peg and Alan were sitting on their terrace after dinner, finishing off a bottle of wine. They were looking at the bungalow and having a whinge about it. "Christian's garage isn't any better, as it happens," said Peg. "But, thankfully, we can't see that as well from here."

Then, Alan, emboldened by an extra glass or two, had suddenly exploded: "I'm going to buy a can of spray paint tomorrow. I'll go down there tomorrow night and spray *Hommes* and *Dames* either side of the bloody door," he said. "It looks like a public convenience!"

When Peg recounted this conversation to Christian (though not her opinion of his garage), he roared with laughter. Ever since, the bungalow has been known by both families as *Les Chiottes* (The Shithouse)! It's less visible now that we've planted shrubs and trees to hide it. Andrée Vermalle and her son Francis come from Marseille to Ribes every July. The only time we ever see her is at the baker's van in the morning, where she buys a *flute* every day, and we exchange chat about the weather and such. Otherwise, she stays indoors. Albert, who has another house in the village, which he inherited with his sister, comes by fairly regularly, but shouts and arguments can usually be heard soon afterwards. Francis, currently fifty, described by the locals as *simple,* looks after the house and 'garden'. Last year, we watched in amazement as he washed the entire house and roof with a high pressure hose! (Not much chance of it ever mellowing or blending in either then!) I'm sure Napoleon meant well when he conceived the inheritance laws – at least brothers **and** sisters inherited equally – but it does create a lot of problems, as properties and land become divided and sub-divided to the point of ridiculousness. We can only look on the positive side. It could be heaps worse – two storeys high and a much noisier family there all the time!

My parents had already suffered another building 'outrage' by a neighbour in 1969 (see photos on page 88). The property in the apex of our L-shaped house, another inheritance 'casualty' – a tiny, no longer useful building – was originally just a simple, two-storey *grange*, used for storing hay, chickens and rabbits. Monsieur Mettayer was renting it from its owner, Monsieur Gevaudan, who gave him permission to increase it a storey, to make more space as he was getting married. In those days, no planning permission was required; people just did what they wanted with their properties. And affluent times had not yet arrived in the Ardèche, so things were often done on the cheap and with not a lot of skill. Peasants pretty much everywhere are famous for their thrifty ways!

This extended wall – I call it *La Bête du Gevaudan* – not only looks dreadful from our side, I doubt whether Monsieur Gevaudan ever came round to see the mess of a construction he gave the go-ahead to. He's no longer around, but The Wall has been a pain for over thirty years. I'm afraid I curse him silently every time I look up at it, especially since it turned into such a nice little earner for him, selling it as he did to Albert from Alsace for nearly £30,000, which in the early nineties here was a lot of money. The extension was so poorly and badly built with no tiles at the edge of the roof. When it rains heavily, the new wall of breeze-blocks covered in a thin render, soaks up water like a sponge, and it eventually trickles down inside *la clède* below. This didn't bother my parents that much because:

a) it didn't rain a lot the time they were here (that is, May to September); and

b) *la clède* was then only used first as a store and later, as extra, rather basic, summer holiday accommodation. Now we're living here longer, it's another matter. We notice the drips!

Since Mike did the roof in 1995 and it continued to leak, it has haunted him whenever it rains. We've been up there time and time again to check, reinforce the fillet, point the stones, and finally spray the entire offending wall with a sealant. This last solution stopped the leak to such an extent that we knew our theory was right and that it really was the fault of The Wall, not the roof. When told about our problem, neighbours wouldn't comment on our opinion about the cause. Mr Gevaudan was rarely in residence. When Albert from Alsace and his wife, Jeanne, moved in – the place had been empty a while after Mr Mettayer's death – we told him about the problem, as he's half responsible for the party wall. He'd simply appeared not to hear or understand – this is quite common! As **he** had no trouble with leaks, the problem didn't exist. (I can sympathise to a certain extent – he didn't cause it, after all.) When we talked to him about the possibility of putting a chimney in, which would have to go against this wall, he was quite amicable about that – it didn't involve him in doing anything – but when I mentioned the wall again, he shut down once more! We give up! Our efforts have been worthwhile, since we've more or less stopped the leak. We are now waiting for Albert to have his roof redone – it must need it soon – and, if we're still here, we'll ask for some improvements to be made our side. Until then we have to live with it. Today, it's been raining all day and it's dripping as I write!

The locals' reactions to opinions, differences and changes brought in by outsiders and outside influences do occasionally exasperate me. When my parents bought the house in the early sixties, the land was still being ploughed by oxen. People rarely, if ever, left the area, the *département*, certainly not the country. Travel to other lands and cultures for pleasure is a relatively recent leisure activity. Television has only been commonplace in the last twenty-five years or so. A non-Ardechois female friend, ex-girl-friend to Christian's brother Alain, at a Balazuc family do, once asked me my opinion of the *Ardechois*, adding that she herself found them absolutely charming on the surface, but it you tried to dig a bit deeper, there wasn't a lot there.

"*Je ne creuse pas,*" I said. (I don't dig.) They, in turn, don't dig either. The majority don't appear to be terribly curious about us and hardly ever ask any questions about where we're coming from. I expect they talk about us when we've gone though!

Every summer for two to three months, they are increasingly heavily invaded by foreign holidaymakers, who admittedly provide them with a reasonable income. As well as the tourists, there are more and more northern Europeans buying up the housing stock for second homes and putting up the property prices generally. So vendors are gaining now, but the next generation may well lose out as they struggle to house themselves and their families.

Meantime, however, the *Ardechois* stay pleasant, friendly and helpful throughout the season and the year, and tolerate us all pretty well! Country people do tend to be more conservative; they don't easily accept the new and different. Despite the rise in material affluence, many of the locals hang on to fixed ideas like grim death and seem to maintain an aversion to change, to evolve. There's a good deal of chauvinism from them towards outsiders, that only they, the indigenous ones, have the right solution to country living – the My Way-syndrome. People in isolated communities that haven't really altered that much for centuries are fair game for the media, stoking up ignorance and suspicion – differences and extremes make good copy, even better pictures. Almost an entire village high up on the Ardèche plateau voted for extreme right-wing Le Pen in the last election, simply because they felt threatened – though they obviously weren't, living where they do – by immigrants and the associated problems. At the last French general election, in Ribes, from an electorate of 234, of whom 201 voted, 170 voted for right-wing Chirac, 20 for Le Pen.

Their reaction to outsiders' building and land maintenance is a very good example of this intolerance and we are an obvious target, as they watch what we do. Gardenwise, I feel we have provided an enormous amount of entertainment for them over the years with our efforts – *"Qu'est-ce qu'il est beau, votre jardin. C'est un parc. Il ne pouvait pas être plus beau!"* says Pierre. (Your garden's beautiful, like a park. Real translation: What on earth are you wasting your time on flowerbeds for? Call **that** a vegetable patch!) Perhaps, privately, they grudgingly think that maybe we're not doing so badly. I'd love to believe it. We're getting more and more compliments about it – mainly from outsiders, though! Unfortunately, as the summers seem to be getting hotter and hotter and watering becomes more and more of a chore, I'm beginning to think we're mad trying to make a garden in this climate.

Fires are a huge problem here in summer, particularly this year, as it's been so dreadfully dry. Garden bonfires, consequently, are forbidden from June to September, which is very understandable.[*] This year, we finally had some prolonged rain after the first week in September, and two of our neighbours immediately lit bonfires when it stopped. You're supposed to get a permit from the *mairie*, then ring the *Sapeurs Pompiers* for further permission, but I know they don't bother. I've asked them. They still warn us, though, that the *pompiers* will come and fine us heavily! So, I dial 18. *"Bonjour. Je vois que des gens du village font du feu aujourd'hui après la pluie. Est-ce qu'on peut brûler maintenant?"* (I see some of the people in the village have fires today after the rain. Are we allowed to burn now?)

"Absolument pas, Madame, c'est interdit jusqu'à la fin du mois." (Absolutely not. It's forbidden until the end of the month.) Only for outsiders who ask, apparently! It niggles us – our bonfires, protected by walls, are huge by now and we want to get on with more pruning and the dump won't take garden waste – but we grit our teeth and wait until the end of September.

I do believe that we may at last have swayed the locals a bit with our various constructions, inside and out. This is in large part down to Mike's artistic talents and building skills. They've praised our makeovers, our pergolas, been amazed by our wall-building and drain-digging, been astounded by The Van, a travelling workshop, from which he appears able to fix anything. This is all very manly and acceptable. But, as well as his cakes, Mike can cook virtually anything. He helps clean, he hangs up the washing, in fact, does anything that needs doing. I think in modern jargon, you'd say he's in touch with his feminine side. Women here have called him *"une perle"* (a gem) and some say they want a clone, which doesn't please their husbands too much! They tut-tut at him and chide him jokingly, but they mean it – they don't understand and, bottom-line, they don't actually approve. The brothers Balazuc, Eric and Christian, teased him once when they saw him wearing a sarong round the garden, calling him a Tahitian. I chided them in my turn and said, laughing, *"Non, vous voyez, il n'a pas peur de porter une jupe. Pas comme d'autres hommes que je connais!"* (**He**'s not afraid to wear a skirt, like some men I

---

* I find it incomprehensible that most fires - not only here in France, but elsewhere, in Australia and the States, for example - are apparently started deliberately. The arsonists must be extremely bitter people.

know!) The word *Touché* came to mind! In an attempt to balance things out and up his *machismo* count, he helps with their repairs and maintenance whenever he can. It seems to have done the trick. As I said earlier, Christian has finally declared – so it's official – that Mike is *"un homme exceptionnel."* And on that we all agree – the men too to save face!

Over the years, we've tried to enhance what was already here, property and land-wise. This cannot be said for eight out of nine of our immediate neighbours, who have other priorities!* The fact is that, apart from the unfortunate external building additions to our hamlet already described, our *quartier* (neighbourhood) remains little changed visually since my parents' time! The house adjoining ours, once an extremely fine one**, has become more and more dilapidated over the years. The small part only that's now lived in has much in common with something you'd see in shantytown. The former owner, Jean Pansier (he of the vagrant chickens) didn't have any sanitary arrangements, bar an open cesspit in his cellar, until, in 2000, the commune bought his house and land in an attempt, rumour has it, to save it from becoming the property of his church, Jehovah's Witnesses. He'd already given them just about everything else he owns. Only then was a septic tank installed. He and his sister have the right to live there until his death – Josette, currently aged 74, will then go into a home. Jean's coming up to his eighties and, apart from the bouts of arthritis he complains of, is in brilliant health and can occasionally still be seen clambering up on his roof, fixing leaks by covering them with yet another tile. The two of them are the only neighbours who've been here longer than me. He's extremely pleasant to talk to – just avoid certain issues! Meanwhile, his cellars have become the village *déchetérie* (dump) and it's right next door. Call me a NIMBY, but I'm obviously not keen!*

---

* One exception, our neighbours, the Balazucs opposite, whose house is always *nickel* (pristine), perhaps too much so!

** It has *"une cheminée sarrasine"*, one of only three in the Ardèche, which is listed and has been restored by the national Département des Beaux Arts. We look at it from one of our windows in *la clède*.

Another very traditional area for the locals is food. The Balazucs are game to try anything new or foreign. The others still stick to what they know and, despite the choice offered by the supermarkets (of which I'm not a great fan – who in Europe really needs unripe starfruit all year round?!), continue to buy what they've always bought, grow what they've always grown, eat what they've always eaten, according to the seasons. Marcelle Nicholas puckered up her face when I tried her out on something as innocent as rocket or coriander. I'll whinge in passing that her husband, who's no longer alive, planted a conifer two metres from our border. It's now well over fifteen metres high and blocks most of the sun on our garden and veggie patch all afternoon, to the extent we've had virtually to pollard one of our cherry trees to get some light. There is also her extremely visible but now redundant (for over twenty years) *poulailler* (chicken house) – another typical peasant construction in corrugated iron and chicken wire. They may just knock these things up, but they don't half last!

And so do they! Pierre, Jean, Marcelle and others of their generation are just wonderful for their age, because they're doers, they're so active. Particularly Marcelle, who's eighty-something and still so fit – I tell her she's *une merveille* (a marvel) and she goes all coy! She looks fantastic and amazingly still tends her veg patch herself. We chat whenever we catch sight of each other in our respective gardens and exchange news and preserves, jams and such. She's well aware of her magnificent tree and its effect and always presents us with a huge bag of her cherries.

On balance, we're extremely lucky with our immediate neighbours and enjoy all the local 'colour' they contribute. But, real communication with the long-term residents is more difficult than with outsiders, both French and foreign, not just because of the heavier accent and *patois* (local dialect – a mix of slang and *occitan* – the old language of Languedoc), but because their life experiences are different, less varied. They talk fast, bluntly, make no allowances for your possible lack of comprehension, because they

---

* Another delightful neighbour, Dario (and another Jehovah's Witness), works part-time for the commune keeping the village tidy, overseeing the recycling of rubbish, strimming the verges and so on.

haven't ever had this experience. I honestly can't decide whether I'd like them to acquire similar social (hypocritical?) niceties, just because that's part of my middleclass-ness, or to remain more uncomplicatedly as they are! But even the mayor, in his editorial in the bi-annual *Bulletin Municipal* – summer edition, is asking his commune members to change and get their fingers out a bit more. (After all, you do want the tourists' money, is the unsaid implication.)

"Nous habitons un charmant village. À nous, tous ensemble, à notre niveau, de le rendre encore plus accueillant en plantant ici une fleur, là un arbuste, en rangeant le vieux tuyau rouillé, visible depuis la voie publique, en remontant le bout du mûr écroulé depuis 20 ans ...

"Alors, retroussons nous les "manches"!! (We live in a charming village. It's up to us, together, each as much as we can, to make it even more welcoming, by planting a flower here, a shrub there, by fixing that old rusty pipe which can be seen from the road, rebuilding that wall that's been down for 20 years ... Let's all pull up our sleeves!)

We do our best, Michel, but it's not that easy when you live next to the dump!

Michel Rouvier is our current, youngest ever mayor, described by some as *dynamique*. He's also extremely charming and approachable (and powerful) at a local level. It's a very different set-up from Britain. Being mayor is similarly a status and power symbol, but it's only a part-time job here, and not a middle class one necessarily, certainly not in the country. He can be found at the *mairie* two afternoons and one morning a week, and you can go see him about anything that's bothering you, and he'll give you his time.[*] (We also know him from Balazuc parties – his cousin, Jean-Luc is married to Christian's sister, Ghiselaine. Jean-Luc's mother, Charlotte, I've known for years. Peg used to go and buy milk from her, and I remember, clearly (which is rare for me these days!) visiting one time with Peg and watching a calf being born.) The Balazucs and the Rouviers are two of the village's old families. And that's what really counts. Everyone else is an *étranger*

---

[*] Except in July and August when he's managing his campsite.

(outsider).

For years I gave that word its other meaning – foreigner – being one myself. It's only by talking to other – French – outsiders that I've learnt the real meaning. One of these confirmations came from Georges Delubac, from whom we buy our vegetables. He and his wife Brigitte are both *Ardechois*. They've lived in various places around the *département* and only came to Ribes about ten years ago. Their house is actually opposite the mayor's campsite (and he's none too pleased at all the new chalets that are going up before his eyes!) I was telling him that my parents were the first *étrangers* in the village. *"Nous sommes tous des étrangers, vous savez!"* (We're all outsiders, you know!) was his immediate response. *"Il faut être né ici!"* (You have to be born here.)

At the last mayoral election, *un étranger* had the audacity to stand for the post and challenge the other candidate, Michel Rouvier, over the development of the commune. French, with a German wife, he'd bought a huge house in the village, for which he had big plans as a cultural/conference centre! Needless to say, it was a complete rout. But it didn't end there. Woe betide you if you sided with the *étranger*. The proprietor of the very good and very successful village restaurant, Bernard, another French *étranger*, did. Now half the village is boycotting his restaurant! Keep your head down, if you want to be loved! Which reminds me about the committee meeting on *Tourisme: Perspectives d'avenir* I attended at the *mairie* in October, since Bernard was also there – he has two *gîtes* as well as the restaurant – and he became a target on this occasion too.

I actually wondered why I'd been invited, apart from the fact that I had a *gîte*. But our house is only *secondaire*, I'm an outsider inviting in more outsiders, and I don't have a vote. I had an idea how it would go, but planned to keep a fairly low profile, certainly if any arguments broke out. It was my first experience of French local politics, and I figured it would be much the same as English local politics – as often as not about the self-interests of the people on the committee. I wasn't wrong. Twenty-one people involved in tourism in the commune – *gîtes*, campsites, our local equestrian centre and so on – had been invited to attend. Thirteen turned up.

A small consultancy agency was to carry out a study on future land use in the commune, and a new *Carte Communale* was to be produced, showing which areas would be allotted to *urbanisme* (new buildings) and which should stay green for agriculture.

The majority at the meeting were adamant that it was no longer possible to make a decent living off the land. They seemed happy with the returns they were making out of tourism and saw the future in terms of more *gîtes*, more and enlarged campsites. My only question to them was how long they could let for. Those who let to outsiders – mainly Belgian and Dutch, but also increasingly German and Swiss – said six months; those who let to the French, only three. Bernard was the only one there who could see beyond his own enterprise and was capable of having a wider, overall view. He'd attended, he said, as a *"citoyen de Ribes"* to discuss a general policy for the commune. He was of the opinion that there could be, that it was vital there should be, a good balance of both activities – tourism and agriculture. It was essential, for example, for residents and visitors to be able to buy good local produce – goat cheeses, decent vegetables, organic poultry and so on, and he supported and bought from local producers. People should diversify, have several strings to their bow; besides it made for more interesting lives. Bigger campsites, more bungalows and visitors who only shopped at supermarkets were not the best solution. I'm in full agreement, but kept my mouth shut. (Call me cowardly if you wish, but I still don't want to rock the boat here. I don't feel I should, even though everywhere else I usually do!) What the participants of the previous meeting, the agriculturists, had come up with, I know not, bar the fact that Monsieur Balmelle, the goat farm owner, left angrily before the end. Bernard's words, too, all fell on stony ground. He finally, unfortunately, also stormed out of the meeting in anger, saying: " *OK, faites encore de vos bungalows. Quand la qualité de vie finira par tellement baisser à Ribes, je m'en irai."* (Build more bungalows, then, but when the quality of life drops too far, I'll be off.) And it was obvious, although a few polite protests were made for him to return, that no-one else was on his side. Although the French are all citizens, as opposed to us Brits who are still royal subjects, both Bernard (and I) get the feeling that the concept of citizenship (is it a middle class one?)[*], or a general responsibility for others, doesn't appear to carry much weight here – there's very little *intérêt commun* in evidence, more *intérêt personnel* or *familial* – it's every man (family) for himself. Very few can see beyond the easy money that tourism brings – what's new? The meeting droned on for about two hours, the comments drifting objectivelessly along. Michel, the mayor, not wanting to offend anyone – rule number one in politics – was not an accomplished chairman and it wasn't kept on course. What's new again? And can you blame them? People will never be told and have to live the experiences of others themselves, before continuing with, or rejecting, them. We will know the outcome for land use in two years' time when the report comes out. Meantime, all new construction permits have been put on hold because of the serious water situation this summer.

In 2001 the whole of the Ardèche, bar two communes who voted to opt out, became the *Parc Naturel Régional des Monts d'Ardèche* (which means it's official – the option of easy money tourism really is the future. Here, just like everywhere else!) With its formation, have come new modernisations and changes in the village. Tasteful walls to hide village dustbins, more tasteful walls to form a parking lot ("paved Paradise" – Joni wouldn't approve and neither do I!) opposite the village hall, road widening, white lines, new signs saying '*Centre Bourg*'. Ribes doesn't **have** a centre; it's spread all over the mountainside, and it's never been a **bourg** before! So much of the change seems to reek of 'corporate identity'. (And to be for the benefit of cars. But, then again, people in the country are very car-dependent.) Many people are putting fences around their properties and ornate gates, and *Propriété privée* and *Défense d'entrer* signs are appearing more and more. As are swimming pools. It's getting like the suburbs. This kind of development comes with growing affluence, of course, for the locals. It's only the outsiders who want to keep it in aspic!

Another aspect of the water business that's distressing me more

---

* According to Jeff, our oracle on many things, especially history, the French Revolution was not engineered by the working-class but by the middle-class.

and more is the whole question of swimming pools. These have been the latest fad in the Ardèche for a while now, and pool suppliers and installers are making big money. I've never liked them much personally – the chlorine, even peroxide, plays havoc with my sinuses and, much more seriously, with the environment[*]. (Now they've had to put chlorine in the tap water as well for a while – this year, for the first time, we were told not to drink our water from the village reservoir.) Until now, there hadn't been many pools in Ribes itself – one in Michel's campsite and a few in Belgian *gîtes* higher up the mountain. In the last few months of this year, however, with the river water even more in question, three of our near neighbours have installed them. And this is probably only the beginning. And it has to be the wrong answer. (I went to Goa in India in 1977/8; lived with an Indian family in a house near the beach. Now it's full of golf courses – those greens have to be watered – and hotels with pools, of course. No longer any water in the wells of the local Indians, though.) The neighbours tell us we must use their new pools. But will we? It's a matter of principle. If we decline, they'll think we're crazy, and we'll be shooting ourselves in the foot if there's no river alternative. Of course, a moral stand won't make any difference to anything. What will we say if the Ardèche becomes third world? Told you so?!

So, that's the pessimistic, bad news! We need some good news to get back to a better equilibrium here. There are days in Ribes, and they are extremely numerous, that are just simply perfect. The garden has been watered naturally and has responded magnificently – all growing things are happy. The weather has turned overnight with the arrival of the north wind. The air is clear; the sunlight on all the vegetation, especially in autumn, is awesome. Whether by the river, in the garden, or walking or mushrooming in the woods, you feel truly at one with all that's around. Simple

---

* If I can quote Trev in Chris Stewart's sequel to *Driving over Lemons*, *A Parrot in the Pepper Tree* (both Sort Of Books, 1999 and 2002): "Aerosols and fridges and bovine flatulence are good for the ozone layer compared to what the chlorine in people's swimming pools is doing. It's the very bane of the planet."

pleasures are enough – *Eschalier's* lemon tarts and Earl Grey tea, enjoying the last of the sun's rays in the garden (it leaves us early in autumn). It's still far too soon to go inside. Let's walk up the mountain a bit, where it's still shining, check out progress on Ghiselaine's and Jean-Luc's new house, being built just a couple of hundred metres above us. (Their family's been living near Valence for the last twenty years but they'll soon be moving back.) What a view they have, overlooking the village below and the mountains stretching away into the distance. Orane comes past in her car on the way up to her new house. She pulls over to talk.

"*Alors, il est venu enfin, le carreleur?*" I ask. (Has the tiler been then?) "*Oui.*" She looks radiant. "*C'est fini. C'est nickel. Je prends une semaine de congé pour déménager.*" (Yes, it's finished. It's brilliant. I'm taking a week off to move in.)

"*Tu montes au Puech? On peut t'accompagner?*" (You going there now – Puech is the name of her *quartier* – can we come too?) "*Bien sûr. Venez voir le carrelage*"

We get in and drive the last kilometre or so, on newly tarmac-ed roads. "*C'est nouveau,*" we comment. "*Oui, ils l'ont fait jusqu'à chez moi. Après, y'a que des maisons secondaires et ça s'arrête net.*" (They've done up to my place. After that, there are only summer houses, so it just stops.) Her house is lovely and beautifully furnished. Everything new. Roberte has had a major hand in this, we know. What a gift for a single, twenty-three year old.

We walk down again. The valley is still bathed in sunshine; the vines are starting to turn red. How the village is changing, I think. But, as we stop to look down on it all, and get the macro view, it hasn't actually changed very much at all. I realise I'm having the same sentiments as Peg at the end of *Lilac and Roses*.[*] You get too involved and bogged down in the micro – the niggley things that bug you, sometimes on a daily basis. But, when you stand back and view the whole – From A Distance – you realise just what you've got. We are so lucky to have so much space, peace and

---

[*] She too talked of changes in the village. But whereas she was bemoaning the loss of friends in Ribes, many people, particularly the Balazucs, are coming back. Vladia, Ludo and Louna are next to build their new house behind Orane's. It's becoming a family ghetto!

warmth, so much in our lives. There is so little we want for. I'm thinking that a place with open space and few people is probably the last great luxury on earth.

Rural France has a reputation of dying in the winter months. This is one thing that **is** actually changing for the better! In October, we had a week-long international film festival in Aubenas. Britain was represented by Stephen Frears – in person! We actually met him! And saw several of his films, including his latest, Dirty Pretty Things. Soon after, in Paysac, there was a three-day music festival with bands playing some extremely interesting 'new' and 'world' sounds ... this is manna from heaven! All this and more besides! Here are more positive aspects of our life here:

- We have a great surrogate family across the road
- We have ever-changing 'neighbours' – most of our guests are very nice indeed
- Lucky's still here, looking cute wherever she choses to put herself, and winning everyone over
- We have beautiful weather most of the time, especially in spring and autumn
- The garden looks lovely most of the year and we get a lot of compliments. I really enjoy looking after it; Mike, too, though he's more a house person!
- The wine's still cheap and good
- We eat well – lots of fresh, organic fruit and veg, lots of fish rather than meat (though we do love the local *saucisson*). If it's true that you are what you eat, therefore, we **are** well on the whole. Our bodies may be drooping, but not our spirits too often.
- We're our own bosses the majority of the time. I still can't get over the fact that we can wake up most mornings and say "What shall we do today?" We always find something and it's usually fulfilling.
- We live in a virtually crime-free zone[*]. We never lock cars; we can go out and not worry about locking things away, not even if

---

[*] In mid-November this year, there were three burglaries in the village - youngsters, apparently, raiding cellars for tools - to sell probably. This is not the news you want to hear when you're on the point of leaving the house empty for a few months!

we leave for a few days. We have no gates or fences around the property and hope we never need to have.

And, as Mike keeps reminding me, "It's a good life, Jan. It's A Wonderful, Wonderful Life!"

It is. Thank you once again, Peg and Alan. We hope you like what we've done to the old pile! Though, I expect we'll do more; it's never really finished, is it?

UPDATE 2004

Hatches and Matches

Joël and Christine Balazuc had a baby girl, Ambre, the day after we arrived in March 2004.

Our Canterbury neighbour and friend, David, who with infinite patience has always fixed our inherited, and therefore problematic, computers in both countries, last visited us at La Clède in 2003 with his *nouvelle amie*, Isabelle. They were married in Caen in November 2004 and expect a baby daughter in February 2005.

Mike's daughter, Clare is marrying Phil on 1 May 2005, not in Las Vegas like her sister, but in Oxford.

Weather

If you were put off the idea of holidaying in the south of France after the big heat in 2003, you might like to know that the weather this summer was totally different. June was not too hot, and we had cool breezes making the evenings fresh. There was even some sustained rain in July and August, in fact, violent storms in August. They started just after the 'official' end to the French holidays, and it rained hard on and off for three days. Nobody, including the locals, could believe the amount of water that was pouring down (on our inside wall too, of course!) Nearly everyone had leaks actually; it's almost unavoidable with that much rain and wind. The river Beaume rose nearly three (the Ardèche nearly six) metres in places, and they flooded their banks, causing great damage to agricultural land and a complete landscape change to our favourite beach. And sadly a death too. A couple camping *sauvage* (ie not in a campsite) on the bank were swept away – the man survived; the woman's body was later found many kilometres down river. The rain continued until the end of the month, when the early morning temperatures dropped down to 13°C – so suddenly autumn! It certainly is a climate of extremes. We didn't entirely escape watering the garden, of course. Before all this, we still had to hump buckets of recycled water around. (It's actually very good exercise; when we're past it, we'll buy a pump!)

Property

Our first guests of the year were seriously house-hunting with a budget of 90,000 euros. During their week's stay with us in April they viewed fifteen properties, none of which was exactly what they wanted, being in disappointing locations and having no land at all at that price. They returned for another go at the beginning of June, found "the right one" (with a roof terrace) and started what proved to be fairly difficult and long legal negotiations. But Jo is fluent in French which certainly helps[*], and by the end of 2004, they told us they were pretty certain that it would be theirs and that the deal would be finalised by February 2005.

This 'invasion' of France by northern Europeans continues apace and TV Relocation/Property as Investment programmes like those in the UK add fuel to the fire. It's hardly an exaggeration to say that a lot of the west of France has been almost colonised, to the point where foreigners/second homeowners are now so numerous that certain mayors are beginning to say Enough, No More! Like most things in life, it's not black and white. Many of the French don't seem to be keen on old properties, preferring new, low-maintenance houses, and in certain areas the outsiders have breathed new life into dying villages. It's the rise in prices for **all** property that causes the grievance. As usual, too much jumping on the bandwagon and not enough balance

---

[*] But it's not essential. Another English couple we've met in the Ardèche arrived in Montelimar in 1998, speaking no French at all and having sold up everything in the UK. They'd chosen the location because they both liked this particular nougat chocolate in the Black Magic selection – seriously! The first estate agent they found showed them the house they now live in. They fell in love with the property and location as soon as they saw it and said they'd buy it without even going inside! Their hunches were right – it's a beautiful house and they are extremely happy with their new life. It's not always quite so easy as that these days!

and moderation. Even around us, we are now aware of a potential backlash. I was jokingly asking some of our neighbours this year if they thought France might reintroduce the *guillotine* for foreign property owners! In fact, the French government, quite rightly, is just aiming to get a slice, through taxation, of revenue generated by their holiday lets.

Prices in the Ardèche have risen about 30 per cent over the last five years and properties are selling like hot cakes. In Ribes, André Vermalle's (of *Les Chiottes*) house was bought by a Parisian doctor within three days of being on the market. The Balazuc brothers sold their mother's house – *"J'ai honte du prix qu'on a reçu,"* said Christian (I'm ashamed of the price we got). Good luck to them; they all work seriously hard.

The continuing saga of Nippi 'n' Nigel

Which brings me on to someone who doesn't seem to rate hard work – Nigel! His Indian restaurant in Laurac, *L'été indien,* is no more. When I rang *Le Relais Fleuri* in June and spoke to the *gardien*, I got the following news:

- The restaurant is back with French cuisine – *c'est la meilleure, n'est-ce pas?* he said! – but is only open during July and August, and he advised booking a week ahead.

- Nigel has a new French girlfriend; apparently, he prefers French women. (That's because they can't tell what a complete plonker he is! – I didn't say that.)

- Raisa **has** bought a house in the area. I've asked Orane, who's a friend of Manu, the estate agent, to find out where, but she's yet to come back to me on this. In fact, there was a distinct lack of interest from our neighbours in the whole story. They vaguely remembered something about an elephant last summer! It's amazing we didn't get any news of what was going on in Laurac last year – that's how local things can be!

Whether Nigel will fulfil his ambition to be mayor of Laurac will presumably be revealed in the next series – if there is one!

Entertainment

We have French TV, which I heartily recommend for improving

French, but great news for us was that cinemas in Aubenas now show original versions (with French subtitles) of many more of the latest films (apart from blockbusters which aren't our thing on the whole). Dubbed movies just aren't the same. So we go often and thus feel far less deprived of our culture! Some goodies this year: The Girl with the Pearl Earring, Coffee and Cigarettes, Lost in Translation, Fahrenheit 9/11 (which won the Palme d'Or, Cannes 2004), 21 Grammes, Super Size Me and Just One Kiss.

Vide-greniers (the equivalent of car boot sales, literally attic-empty-ers), are really taking off in a big way, as happened in England. There's at least one every week within striking distance. New friend Maggie, who's bought a barn to convert near Les Vans, and is furnishing/ equipping it with the help of these events, gloomily predicts they will lead to a similar increase in petty theft crime. Not for a while yet, we hope, and we still don't lock house, cellars or cars (when parked *chez nous*).

Mini-hols

In May we had one of our great little trips, exploring this time in the *Parc National des Cévennes* – wild mountain/river country – with the help of an article from Living France magazine (Issue 125, Sept 2002). We camped in the forest near the summit of its highest mountain, Aigoual, and awoke with very cold bottoms in the morning – a tad chilly at over 1,200 metres! As usual, we spent our days seeing wonderful sights like the stunning Cirque de Navacelles and the standing stones and dolmens on the Causse de Blandas, the beautifully restored mill at La Foux, where the river Vis, after 6kms underground, comes thundering out of a huge fissure in the rocks, at its most powerful at some thirty cubic metres a second! A somewhat warmer two nights in the valley of the Arre in a lovely campsite just outside Le Vigan – fantastic Musée Cévenol there. On to extremely medieval Sumène, where the last silk factory is still in business, up the Rieutord river to Saint Martial and the Corniche. The scenery is just superb and we never tire of it.

Bernadette, our teacher friend from Les Vans needed our help again to move herself and her stuff for *la rentrée* (the new school year) back to Nice. Another driver had driven into her in town, and her car had been written off by *l'expert*. It would seem that French insurance companies are no more reasonable than British ones when push comes to shove, ie when you put in a claim (especially during the month of August!) We agreed we would drive her to Avignon, and her cousin Guy, now retired as chief of police, would pick her up from there. It meant we could spend the day getting another culture fix!

It was our first trip to Avignon centre (I'd only ever visited the *grandes surfaces* – the commercial and industrial zones that now encircle every town of any size in France – to buy equipment for the house). The old part within the city walls is delightful with far too many museums and galleries for one short visit. We were real tourists and did the Popes' Palace and the famous bridge. Then the fabulous Musée Angladon, a private art and craft collection started by fashion designer Jacques Doucet in the 1920s and '30s, and inherited and added to by engravers/painters, Jean Angladon and his wife Paulette Martin. The collection, in their beautifully renovated former home, comprises original paintings by Van Gogh, Picasso, Modigliani and the like, as well as some stunning Chinese antiques. Especially one, and how I coveted it! A terracotta figure of a dancer, some 37cms (15″) high from the beginning of the Tang dynasty (618 – 907), which was simply exquisite. Standing there admiring it, I couldn't help thinking about the theft of The Scream!! All you need is the bottle, but I don't have it, unfortunately!

We decided, since we were so close, to go on into the Camargue, somewhere else neither of us has been, but unfortunately it was a dreadful mistake. It is just so touristy in August and, of course, everywhere was pricey and full. The town of Saintes Maries de la Mer on the coast was so full of people, we didn't even bother to get out of the van and rapidly drove off north again, homeward bound, dismayed at the endless number of places offering *Promenades à cheval*. How tired and bored those poor horses looked. They were all 'regulation' white, and we did also see lots of marshland, complete with bulls and flamingos, so I guess you could say we've 'done' it!

Halfway back, we stopped for a meal at the town of Sommières, which was so badly hit by the flooding of the Gardon a couple of years ago. It's all been beautifully restored now, and we wandered through the lovely old town, looking for a likely restaurant. La Bistoure seemed quite promising. A new business by the look of it, with the interior, especially the toilets, extremely stylishly architect-designed. The disappointing meal (getting more and more typical these days, it seems) was tepid, ie not microwaved long enough; *'nouvelle cuisine'* portions on giant plates, brought to the table before bread and wine (another five minute wait). As we paid our bill, we were asked if we'd enjoyed it.

"WC super", I retorted, *"bouffe moyenne!"* (Lovely loos, shame about the food!)

Some village news

At the beginning of the season, we read with interest that, according to the tourist office publication, *Herbergements 2004* (Where to stay), our mayor, Michel, was charging 728 euros a week in high season for one his new, plastic-looking chalets (for a family of four, with air conditioning and dishwashers!). These were obviously a large investment for him, but I'm afraid he found himself with a half-empty campsite in July. Tourists were generally down this year, notably in July, though happily not *chez nous*! As has happened on the Côte d'Azur (now 'owned' in large part by the Russian mafia, we're told), most accommodation and catering providers are out-pricing themselves. The French, in particular, are simply going elsewhere. There are now, of course, the additional unspoiled attractions of the far cheaper eastern European countries that have come into the Union. (I'll put in a plug for La Clède here – it's much more private, spacious, comfortable and less expensive than a chalet! See ad further on.) To add injury to insult, the night of the violent storm (17th August), Michel had to open up the village hall to provide shelter for all his poor sodden campers.

Charging around on quad bikes is the latest sport. Christian and brother Eric couldn't resist spending some of their house-sale money on a new toy each and bought hunting green ones (naturally!); our mayor, has a bright red one – to be seen (also naturally!)

(Christian, by the way, no longer has to commute to Crédit Agricole, Coucouron on the plateau; he's been transferred to Les Vans, a mere twenty minutes away and is so much the better, and less stressed, for it. Happy neighbours are the best!)

The first *Journée des Peintres* (Painters' Day) took place in the village in late June. Some two dozen local amateur artists, at the invitation of our mayor, spent the day spread around Ribes, drawing whatever took their fancy, building and landscape-wise – together with the mandatory socialising of course. What with coffee and cake at 9am, being wined and dined by the commune at lunchtime (90 minutes minimum) and an *apéro* over an exhibition of the work at 7pm, they had barely more than a few hours actual painting! Three of them came to our hamlet and one, our friend Renée, painted our house. Another friend, Béa Cachelou, who teaches art in Joyeuse, did a lovely watercolour of the alley between us and the Balazucs and very kindly presented it to us afterwards. I did a laser colour-copy for our neighbours. Unbeknown to us, Christian had seen it in the exhibition and had tried to buy it, but it already had a red sticker (*vendu* – to us!) He was therefore delighted to be presented with a framed copy! It was a highly social and interesting day, albeit an extremely hot one – I think Bea was so grateful for the parasol and drinks we provided! I really hope it becomes an ongoing event.

In the summer edition of our bi-annual *Bulletin Municipal,* there was a feature on our neighbour Pierre, to be 78 this year.

"Qui ne connaît pas 'Pierrot', son caractère trempé, son timbre de voix si caractéristique et sa gouaille inimitable?!!!" (Who doesn't know Pierrot with his even-tempered character, his unmistakable voice and unique banter.) His biggest regret? The lack of life in the village these days – fewer young people, fewer farming folk and businesses (no longer a resident baker or a shop, but we do have a travelling baker/grocer, a tourist office, a library and an art gallery, none of which the locals are particularly enamoured with!) It's not through your lack of trying to inject some life, dear Pierre! Interestingly enough, in the In Short section of the bulletin,

was this little item:

"Vivre en bon voisinage
Les plaintes les plus fréquentes sont liées au bruit, mais également
aux chiens ..."

(Good neighbourliness
The most frequent complaints are about noise and dogs ...)!!
We are not alone then!

In the mid-nineties, Ribes received an award from the then Minister of the Environment for its striking terrace walls and vineyards, plus a grant for the removal of some of the electricity pylons. More such works began in the village in September around our hamlets, Gelly, Plôt and Fabre. There were huge reels of cable, piles of gravel and diggers everywhere, and teams of men working from 8am to 6pm, so Pierre revelled in all the extra 'life' going on around him, and his dogs had a field-day, adding their noise to all the rest. We left before the work was finished and eagerly look forward to next spring and our pylon-free views.

Visitors

We had another season of very pleasant guests in the *gîte,* and lots of visits from family members staying with us, which is always a great pleasure: Louise and Lawrence twice, the second time with Lawrence's mum, niece Molly and friend, Susie, followed by Clare and Phil, and brother Ian and Tina at the end of September. The weather throughout was lovely – day after day of sunshine – and we spent a great deal of time at the river, which we often had to ourselves. The big storm in August had changed part of our favourite beach from sand to pebble, and the course of the water flows. On the far side there was still a deep pool, perfect for swimming and larking about in but rather murky, as the main river flowed straight past it. With an undeterred Mike in charge, we created a rapid down into it, all of us spending hours chucking rocks and stones onto either side to form the banks of a new channel. Going down it on an inflated lilo was just enormous fun, ending in a beautiful, newly clean swimming pool. What a transformation, but what a shame it won't last, as the winter rains will change it all again! Our Czech friends visited us too and we all skinny-dipped there on 24 September. Mike and I again on the last day of the month, the latest dip ever. It was a bit *fraîche* but just divine and of course we were entirely alone.

Maxi hols

We left Ribes on 10 October (the earliest for years) and it was a real wrench. The weather was still lovely, the garden still full of flowers and vegetables – even strawberries – which we told the neighbours to help themselves to, of course. Mike and I were flying off, via Hong Kong (out) and Bangkok (back), to spend nearly two months in Australia, crossing the continent from Perth to Sydney, via Adelaide and Melbourne. The holiday of a lifetime. First stage across the desert on the Indian-Pacific railway and then in a camping car, driving round the coast road to Sydney. In Western Australia, we stayed with Tony and Trish who were guests at La Clède in 2002. In Adelaide, we met up with a friend Scott (former flatmate from London), who gave me the title of this book, and in Sydney we were guests of Mike's daughter Lauren and her new partner, Guy. The word marriage was mentioned! Which is where we came in this year. Watch this space…

CEVENNES/ARDECHE
Village Farmhouse, 18thC, Sleeps 4+, Ideal two couples
- Restored period stone farmhouse on hillside of conservation village – Ribes, near Joyeuse (30km to Ardèche Gorges)
- Spacious (100m²), comfortable holiday home-from-home with beams and traditional country furniture
- Sunshine, calm, beautiful mountain views, lovely river swimming and sports activities nearby
- For walkers, cyclists, artists, nature-lovers, sightseers, food and wine fans
- Two double bedrooms + twin bed space, shower room/WC + bathroom/WC, large lounge/diner + kitchen/diner (washing machine and dishwasher)
- Exclusive use of two furnished terraces (one covered), built-in barbecue
- Large, terraced garden with secluded sitting areas in sun and shade
- Courtyard parking
- Prices inclusive, except linen and heating, if required.

Lets from Easter to Christmas/New Year (discounts available)

For photos and more information:
Jan Bevan. Tel: 07814 792118 or 00 33 4 75 39 56 97

LA CLÈDE – VISITORS' COMMENTS

We've had some wonderful comments in our Visitors' Book over the years. Here are a few from 2003:

"The most comfortable, spacious and well equipped accommodation we have ever had in France. The garden is a delight." (May)

"We thought the house lovely, so thoughtfully appointed ... What a beautiful part of France you live in; the scenery is stunning." (June)

"We have enjoyed our stay at La Clède; it is like home from home and so well equipped. You have a lovely garden with superb views." (June)

"La Clède is everything you dream about in finding/booking/staying in a self-catering property. Its charm/high standards/position put it right up there with the very best places we have stayed in France." (July)

"The gîte is as lovely and clean and welcoming as ever – La Clède has become home from home for us." (July – sixth visit)

"One of the best gîtes we've stayed in. Great welcome, pristine home, fantastic garden." (September)

"Super to go into a house and feel that no-one has just left and been there before." (September)

"It is hard to leave; we are just becoming used to this great life in delightful surroundings. Your gîte is so special – no wishing you'd brought so and so – it's all here, set in a beautiful garden." (September)

"This area of France is a little bit of heaven on earth. Peace and quiet, amazing scenery and one of the most beautifully cared for houses we have stayed in. Everything has been carefully thought out ... and the whole holiday experience is a joy. We shall be most sorry to leave." (September)

This is the nicest rented accommodation – and best equipped – that we have had – a real home from home to return to." (October)

THANK YOUS

1: for coming back and being much more than guests, to:

Roger and Gill (the winners with six visits!)
Andrew and Mary (second with four)
Richard and Diane
Peter and Virginia
Milan and Bella
Roger and Mon
Eric and Liz
Pete and Chris
John and Joyce
Mike and Barbara, and
Jeremy (second time with Kate - All The Way From America)

2: to Mike for putting up with me while I was writing this and for his contributions in editing it.

3. finally, to the "Living Treasure", Joan Anderson, for the gifts of her words, music and paintings. I list all her albums opposite.

JONI MITCHELL'S ALBUMS

Song To A Seagull (Reprise, 1968)
Clouds (Reprise, 1969)
Ladies Of The Canyon (Reprise, 1970)
Blue (Reprise, 1971)
For The Roses (Asylum, 1972)
Court And Spark (Asylum, 1974)
Miles Of Aisles (Asylum, 1974, live)
The Hissing Of Summer Lawns (Asylum, 1975)
Hejira (Asylum, 1976)
Don Juan's Reckless Daughter (Asylum, 1977)
Mingus (Asylum, 1979)
Shadows And Light (Asylum, 1980, live)
Wild Things Run Fast (Geffen, 1982)
Dog Eat Dog (Geffen, 1985)
Chalk Mark In A Rainstorm (Geffen, 1988)
Night Ride Home (Geffen, 1991)
Turbulent Indigo (Geffen, 1994)
Hits (Reprise, 1996, compilation)
Misses (Reprise, 1996, compilation)
Taming The Tiger (Reprise, 1998)
Both Sides Now (Reprise, 2000, compilation)
Travelogue (Reprise, 2002)*
Dreamland (Warner, 2004, compilation)

*"This is, quite simply, a quantum masterpiece. Joni is at the peak of her powers. Even her paintings seem to me to be especially revelatory, gathered as they are in the sleeve. Someone told me that she plans no more recording. If she never made another record, this one will stand as a testament not only to her work, but to the greatness of American orchestral music".
From Pete Townsend's (of The Who) website, 2004

ONLY·WHEN THE LAST· TREE·HAS·DIED·& THE LAST·RIVER HAS BEEN·POISONED & THE LAST·FISH HAS BEEN·CAUGHT WILL·WE·REALISE·THAT·WE·CAN-NOT·EAT·MONEY·

19TH CENTURY CREE INDIAN

"Cannot eat money", quote from an anonymous 19th century Native American. Design: Kate Charlesworth and Grafica. Cath Tate Cards, PO Box 647, London SW1 4JX, www.cathtatecards.com